BLACK
GHOSTS

Also by Noo Saro-Wiwa

Looking for Transwonderland: Travels in Nigeria

BLACK GHOSTS

A Journey Into the Lives of Africans in China

NOO SARO-WIWA

CANONGATE

First published in Great Britain, the USA and Canada in 2023
by Canongate Books Ltd, 14 High Street, Edinburgh EH1 1TE

Distributed in the USA by Publishers Group West
and in Canada by Publishers Group Canada

canongate.co.uk

1

British Library Cataloguing-in-Publication Data
A catalogue record for this book is available on
request from the British Library

ISBN 978 1 83885 694 6

Typeset in Garamond Premier Pro by Palimpsest Book Production Ltd,
Falkirk, Stirlingshire

Printed and bound in Great Britain by Clays Ltd, Elcograf S.p.A.

To all the African immigrants around the world
who are striving against the odds

CONTENTS

I

A FETCHING DESTINATION

The three of us were gathered around a counter, eyeing pornographic imagery. A Chinese vendor, a veiled-up Muslim lady from Niger, and me. We were standing in a low-lit corridor in the Tianxiu Building in the city of Guangzhou, among a series of mildly shabby market-style stalls piled high with bottles and boxes that bore photos of oiled flesh and lustful eyes promising pleasure and endurance. I and the Chinese man looked on as his Nigerienne customer inspected a box of aphrodisiac pills, its packaging displaying a photo of a man (with what I pray was a prosthetic penis) in session with a naked woman. Seized by embarrassment, my ears grew hot and I developed a phantom itch on my nose. The lady from Niger, however, didn't give a toss. She was here on a shopping mission and had little time to waste on coyness or prudery.

'Many, many,' she told the Chinese seller, using the international phrase for wholesale purchasing. The lady ordered a thousand packets of 'Brother Long Legs', secured a delivery date for the merchandise, then walked off with her friend, chatting away in French.

The Tianxiu Building is a magnet for African wholesale

buyers. Dotted around me were glass counters stacked with all manner of 'sexuality enhancing' products, sold by Chinese people who stood by nonchalantly while I checked out their merchandise. I saw vagina-tightening gels, 'extra strong delay sprays for long-lasting excitement' and – most intriguing of all – a 'high-grade professional female oestrus induction toner' called Spanish Gold Fly. The packaging of another aphrodisiac had Arabic script printed on it and a photo of a Black man being 'entertained' below the waist by two white ladies. I scarcely knew where to put my eyes. The vendors slouched behind their counters and fiddled with their phones.

Very few things surprise Chinese manufacturers and wholesalers. They are the eyes and ears of the consumer universe. They know all our secrets and desires, and produce for them accordingly. They have the low-down on the condom sizes favoured by various nations; they know which toys our children prefer. One third of all Christmas trees are manufactured here in Guangdong Province in southern China.

There is nothing Chinese vendors haven't seen before. Motivated by an all-consuming desire to make money (this non-Christian nation runs the world's biggest Bible printing press, after all), they were unoffended by my camera and time-wasting inquiries. So long as they made sales at some point in the day I was allowed to snoop, prod and ogle to my heart's content.

And so I checked out 'hip lift' massage creams and hair wigs and Malaysian hair weaves. Some of the Chinese vendors had adopted the African method of hissing to get my attention – 'Hello, my sista,' they said, while showing me buttock-enhancing yansh pads ('yansh' means buttocks in Nigerian slang) and packets of ginseng tea, formulated to strengthen the kidneys, supposedly.

The second floor was the place to buy underwear. Some of the packaging displayed faces of famous footballers that had been photoshopped onto Y-front-clad torsos: an improbably buff Zinedine Zidane showed off his bulge. Buck-toothed Ronaldinho looked especially pleased to be wearing his 100 per cent combed cotton singlet. David Beckham, meanwhile, sizzled in a white vest and briefs, his left hand cupping his crotch. But by far my favourite was the 'Black Power Obama Collection' – a pack of men's underpants decorated with a photo of America's finest president, fingers on chin, eyes gazing eruditely into the distance. In the free-for-all that is the China–Africa small commodity trade, matters of trademark protection and image rights do not enter the equation. Just shift the product.

In 2012 China sold billions of dollars' worth of products to Africa, from bridges and hospitals to flat-screen TVs, wheelchairs, crutches, toilets, sofas, clothes and medical equipment. The country is Africa's largest trading partner, in a relationship that has blossomed since the 1950s when China tried to create ideological solidarity with African countries in order to promote Chinese-style communism and counter Taiwanese, American and Russian influence during the Cold War. China supported independent movements in Africa, provided weapons and military training, and invited African students to study at Chinese universities.

In the 1970s China's then premier, Deng Xiaoping, opened up the country's communist economy to the world. Deng turned the southern province of Guangdong into a free enterprise and manufacturing zone, with Guangzhou as its wholesale and retail centre. Such reforms went against communist ideals, Deng acknowledged, but after the poverty of the Cultural Revolution, the country had to make compromises in order to progress. 'When you open the window,' he proclaimed, 'flies come in.'

By the 2000s, China provided huge loans to Africa when the IMF wouldn't. It built infrastructure projects to replace the haggard modernist monoliths that sprouted in Africa during oil booms and colonial times, plus new bridges, highways, airports, stadiums and presidential palaces. The poorest countries were granted zero tariffs on a sizeable chunk of their exports to China, and in turn, Africans were allowed to go to China and buy the small commodities that our low-manufacturing economies didn't make or had stopped making. Africans began travelling to China, some of them traders on temporary visits, others settling there permanently in what is a relatively recent phenomenon in the history of global migration. For some, this relationship between China and Africa signified the start of a post-colonial epoch, free of Western mediation. No more finger-wagging 'wypipo' on their civilising missions. The Middle Kingdom's refusal to criticise or moralise was music to the ears of the sensitive kleptocrats in Africa. Approving African commentators overlooked the fact that Western governments were under pressure from ethics-minded voters to withhold financial support to foreign governments perceived in those countries as having poor human rights' records. China has no voters to answer to, no human rights standard to maintain; when it offered money without the usual strings, some commentators saw a refreshing simplicity in this deal, this New Amorality.

What China also offered was a chance for Africans to live within its borders or visit on short-term visas in order to buy small commodities and do other business. While Europe closed its doors (the UK even refused entry to a Nigerian woman wanting to donate a kidney to her dying sister), China became a place Africans could visit easily and legitimately. I remember my amazement when I first heard about Africans living over there in the mid-2000s. It seemed such an incongruous concept. Though I was well-travelled, many of the countries I had visited were on the 'Atlantic Rim', where connections between Africa and Europe and the Americas were woven by history and colonialism, which brought cross-pollination and syncretism of religion and language and music: the gods of Brazil's Candomble religion still retain the original names of the Yoruba gods in Nigeria; pidgin English, the creole tongue of Africa, contains words like *pikin* for 'child', which derives from the Portuguese *pequeno* ('small'). It's in our music, those African-American soul melodies with their hints of African call and response, performed in a relatable diatonic music scale. China, by contrast, was a separate and nebulous universe, with its traditional pentatonic music scale and impossible pictographic writing system. The closest I came to China was through school, an all-girls boarding school on England's south coast, which was a magnet for pupils from Hong Kong, Singapore and Malaysia, many of them ethnic Chinese. They taught me words and concepts like *feng shui* and gave exciting accounts of their end-of-term flights to Hong Kong and the aircrafts' precarious landings at Kai Tak airport through a forest of skyscrapers, flying so close to the buildings that one could see people doing the dishes. The following term the girls would bring back delicious packet noodles, which I would beg to buy off them. They taught me how to use chopsticks, though everyone seemed to have a different technique. Tired of watching me struggle, Pia from Hong Kong snatched the sticks out of my hand and fed me herself, thrusting the chopsticks so far into my mouth I gagged and noodles came tumbling out in giggling fits. After her holidays back home in Singapore, Christabelle would celebrate her suntan, stroking her bronzed skin with pride. Some girls had English accents and liked hip-hop as much as I did, and humped the floor like the rest of us when Vanilla Ice's 'Ice Ice Baby' came on the radio. They studied European languages and sang Handel's *Messiah* in choir, and went on to attend British universities. They told me things about Causeway Bay and Kuala Lumpur and Singapore. But mainland China rarely came up in any conversations that I can remember.

The country held a certain mystery. It lacked the accessibility and familiarity of Thailand or Vietnam. People could travel to Southeast Asia without stepping out of their comfort zone, but venturing behind China's Bamboo Curtain required a certain boldness and concentration of mind, especially in the pre-smartphone era. I wanted to experience the country and detangle my mental collage of Burberry raincoats, army tanks, Tiger Moms, modern skyscrapers, government restrictions, economic liberalism, harsh factory conditions and even harsher hair fringes.

My first encounter with a mainlander had done nothing to change the air of mystery. I was at Columbia University in New York in 2000. During an orientation session at my halls of residence everybody was asked to get into pairs and listen to one another's biographies, before relaying their partner's to everyone else in the room. It was supposed to be an ice-breaking conversational exercise, but while the other pairs chatted away genially my Chinese partner whipped out her notepad and took down my age, name and provenance as if she were a cop placing me under arrest.

From what I could see, mainland China had a disdain for certain foreign cultures and was a stranger to political correctness. Traditionally it believed itself to be the 'Middle Kingdom', lying at the centre of the known universe; its old-school palaeontologists theorised that Chinese people evolved separately from the rest of humanity. Its citizens dislike dark skin so much they virtually mummify themselves to avoid getting suntans. Their social media app, WeChat, translates the term *hei gui/hak gwei* ('black ghost', or 'devil') to 'nigger', even though *bai gui/gweilo* is simply translated to 'white ghost'. What was life like for Africans living in a society like this? How did Africans navigate it? I wanted to meet these immigrants. I also wanted to learn more about mainland China itself and see if the frequently mentioned 'developmental parallels' between Africa and China were valid. Could there ever be a fusion of African and Chinese culture? If so, I couldn't picture it.

In my lifetime, I had encountered infinite permutations of the immigrant experience, from Lebanese people in Guinea, to Nigerians who live in Alaska or speak with Scottish brogues. In our economically liberalised and interwoven world, the exotic 'ethnic enclave' has lost its novelty to an extent. But Africans living in China still held a certain intrigue, this Sino-African fault line a relatively new and unlikely bumping of cultural tectonic plates. I wanted to observe that fault line up close and get first-hand experience of their lives as hei gui. Without knowing anybody in Guangzhou, I boarded a plane to Hong Kong and took off into the unknown.

—

Having arrived in Hong Kong, I took a train from Hung Hom station in the Kowloon area to Guangzhou in mainland China. My neighbouring passenger, probably a seasoned traveller on this route, closed the window blinds against the lowering sun and blocked my views of the landscape. I wasn't happy about making such a blind entry into China, but in hindsight the lack of a visual preview made the arrival more impactful.

At Guangzhou East railway station, I emerged onto a dimly lit concrete platform and was hit by an indefinable aroma – something spicy clogging the air, smelling unlike anything I was familiar with. At immigration, a uniformed guard who was significantly younger than me grabbed my attention with a loud clap of his hands and pointed sharply to the correct queue. Smarting at his youth and authoritarian manner, I moved to the line on the far side of the room. Minutes later, I emerged from the station and was dazzled by what I saw. Tall glass buildings, shiny cars, clean, wide roads regulated by traffic lights; a McDonald's gleamed across the intersection opposite me; the iconic Canton Tower, a sensual hourglass structure, loomed futuristically in the distance, all 604 metres of it, against a purple and orange sunset that lent a foreign-planet hue to this cityscape.

Guangzhou's newness was uniform and impressive, and it spoke of a concerted master plan; of a sleeping dragon that had woken up and wiped the crust from its eyes. Frankly, it made a mockery of the notion of any 'developmental parallels' between China and Africa (which, of course, is not a country but matches China in terms of population size).

I settled into a hotel near Ximenkou metro station in the Yuexiu district. When dinnertime came, I stepped out onto the street and inhaled that same aroma. Here the buildings were older-looking, with hardware shops and small restaurants beneath porticos. The foreignness of it all made me want to return to bed and curl up, but hunger has a way of making you adventurous.

I picked out the only restaurant on my street that was still open at 10.30 p.m. Its menu was a million Chinese characters floating in front of my eyes. The only word I knew was 'umgoi', Cantonese for 'thank you'. Pride set in, and I stared at that sea of characters with an affected air of familiarity.

My random selection turned out to be balls of indeterminate meat in a salty soup. A two-year-old girl sitting nearby took one look at my African features and immediately burst into tears (my silver puffer jacket probably added to the extraterrestrial look). I waved at her. When her mother encouraged her to wave back, the toddler paused to observe me properly and her grimace softened into befuddlement as she recognised the humanness of my smile.

Thirty years ago, the kid's mother might also have been horrified by the sight of me. When Africans settled here in the early 2000s, the Chinese thought they 'smelled bad'. Not ones for subtlety, they lurched sideways when an African passed them on the street and plunged their noses in their shirt collars. Some would touch the immigrants and ask, with genuine innocence, 'Why are you black?'

One of the earliest official reports of Africans (diplomats and students aside) coming to China was a group of Kenyan acrobats who had been sent there for training at the request of the Kenyan president, Daniel arap Moi. And, in 1973, China played the US basketball team in an exhibition match in Beijing. In his memoirs the first US Consul General in China, Richard L. Williams, described the moment the Chinese crowd saw a Black person for the first time. The American team's two white players entered the court first, to regular applause. But when the first of the Black players emerged, with his gangly brown limbs and big Afro hair, eighteen thousand Chinese spectators gasped in what Williams dubbed 'the largest mass inhalation ever recorded'.

The current immigration wave (aside from foreign students) began in the 1990s when Malian Muslims arrived in Guangzhou. Some of them had studied in China and decided to stay in the country after graduation. They settled in the Xiaobei neighbourhood, partly because they could buy halal meat from butchers' run by the Uighurs, ethnic Muslims from Xinjiang Province in the northwest.

By 2008, up to twenty thousand Africans were thought to be living in Guangzhou, though nobody knows the exact figures. The biggest concentration of sub-Saharans is still in Xiaobei and the neighbouring Sanyuanli district, in an area known collectively (by the media, at least) as 'Chocolate City'.

—

I wanted to meet some Africans and speak to them, to find out more about their lives in China. So next morning I headed to Xiaobei, where the Tianxiu Building stands. Located by the inner ring road, the building is the ultimate symbol of African China, the Eiffel of the African Orient. Next to it, on the pedestrian bridge, a Chinese photographer was taking photos of Africans posing in front of the building and then selling them the images. She displayed some photographs on easels, male faces grinning at proud angles. The Tianxiu's metallic façade – blue and pink and shimmering with '80s-style brashness – was, to be frank, an ugly thing, but celebrating such a backdrop was fitting for those on the margins of the global economy. When your passport is disdained by consulates the world over, entering China via the front door is the attainment of an otherwise impossible mobility.

The photographer was a short and sprightly woman with a ponytail and parka. The briefest of eye contact was all the prompting she needed to rope me in to posing in front of the building. I didn't resist. Smiling and enthusiastic, she scurried between various staircases and motioned for me to stand this way and that, hands in my pockets, sideways to the camera, etc. My dignity was plummeting with every shot. Still, if I was to look cheesy anywhere on earth then let it be here where nobody knew me. Jaws clenched, I grinned at her lens.

The woman hurried to an ancient-looking printer sitting on a small stand. While it cranked out the prints, a newspaper reporter wandered over, hoping to interview me for a story about Africans in Guangzhou. Born in Nigeria, I told her. British citizen. And a tourist . . . sort of. I didn't fit her desired profile, so she turned to the photographer for a chat instead. Translation: business was down significantly from the previous year. Fewer Africans were coming to Guangzhou.

Minutes later, the photographer handed over the finished low-res prints, which I bought. My face grinned from beneath the hood of my puffer jacket. I looked like any other African immigrant, excited to have reached this destination, ready for this new world, this new experience.

Searching for Africans to talk to, I walked deeper into Xiaobei. The neighbourhood lies next to a large concrete flyover, a spaghetti knot of elevated walkways surrounded by brutalist seventies architecture. On the pedestrian bridge, two dozen Han Chinese moneychangers wielded bricks of cash (said to be scattered with counterfeit notes) and calculated sums on their phones while offering me their services. A few feet away, a Muslim man in a white kufi hat, his limbs splayed grotesquely at all angles beneath him, begged for money. His Muslim brethren, a mélange of kaftaned Turks, Arabs, Pakistanis, Africans and Uighurs fresh from Friday prayers, sauntered past his empty collection bucket.

Friday prayers had just finished, and I was met by the sight of a dozen Uighur men walking slowly along the streets. They were a handsome group, with their Chinese epicanthic eyes and hybrid faces of Central Asia and Persia, looking beautiful in their white thawbs and doppas.

Somewhere in this concrete jungle was the Donfranc Hotel, which is popular with Africans. I was considering moving there and wanted to inspect its rooms, but first I needed to find it. Since Google and its maps are banned in China, the natural thing to do was to ask Africans for directions. But there was something different about the sub-Saharans here. Overwhelmingly male, they didn't stop to offer me unsolicited help as normally happens on the home continent. There was none of the friendly idleness, the sitting on street chairs watching the world go by; no snapping of fingers summoning me to deliver a chat-up line. Such irritating attention would have come in handy now, but people were busy. They were on their phones, counting cash, eyeing merchandise, not wanting to be inconvenienced. Their eyes told me to fuck off. Some even shook their heads pre-emptively as I approached them. Those who did stop to talk turned out to be mostly Francophone, Muslim, somewhat aloof with women and impatient with my rusty French. A nice Ivoirian man finally pointed me in the right direction.

I walked beneath an elevated walkway and emerged on Zhijie Baohan Xiatangxi. Numerous Black people were walking the street. The government's immigration anxiety expressed itself in the form of a police station with sentry post and a swing arm barrier for cars. It didn't take me too long to find the Donfranc Hotel. All the guests in the lobby were Black. Such a melanin-rich environment is clearly too much to handle for some Chinese folks, who articulate their discontent with a frankness bordering on the comical. One online review of the Donfranc, Google-translated, is bluntly titled 'Here are blacks'. Another reviewer doesn't mince words either: 'The hotel facilities are obsolete . . . the rooms are dirty, dimly lit, with no windows inside . . . Guests predominantly black . . .'

I entered the lobby. To my right was a line of Caucasian mannequins dressed in African garb and headscarves. A neon exchange-rate screen hung on the wall and beneath it sat two Chinese receptionists, looking moodier than the moodiest of Nollywood actresses and speaking transactional English and French. The long-haired one dangled a key from her limp wrist. I took it and inspected the room upstairs. Though the accommodation didn't deserve reviews as harsh as some of those found online, the overall vibe still did not impress; I would not be moving here. In the elevator back down, I tried striking up conversation with a tall West African man dressed in shiny robes, but he just frowned at me with disgusted eyes and flared nostrils.

Xiaobei was proving a tough nut to crack, for reasons I came to understand through an email from a Chinese academic contact:

> Xiao Bei Lu and Xia Tang are the places where the African immigrants live and work. I suggest that you rent a place in that area and live for a while, then you can slowly go into the communities. They are very cautious people.
>
> Christians and Muslims are living separately, so are the drug dealers.

Next door to the Donfranc Hotel was the Overseas Trading Mall, another small commodities market frequented by Africans. I bought a beautiful fake Gucci watch and a small rucksack, then floated around the neighbourhood for an hour, not knowing what to do with myself. Guangzhou is an industrial city, and this district was wholesale-oriented, where interactions were more financial than anything else. Unless you had a job or an export business there was little to see and do here. Everything was on sale.

I could think of no pretext to talk to people, and my aimlessness exposed the lie that I was a tourist. Deflated, I headed to the neighbouring district of Sanyuanli a couple of miles to the west of Xiaobei, where the English-speaking Africans were concentrated.

—

I entered the subway station. It was new and metallic and shiny, bilingual signs everywhere. The loudspeaker played muzak, a strangely mournful xylophone-sounding instrument that repeated the same two-bar arpeggio all day. Somehow the uniformed staff tolerated it.

Among the passengers I could pick out Chinese migrants from the countryside, based on certain hairstyles and clothes. One could gauge their freshness by the way in which they navigated the station. The most recent newcomers hesitated at the top of the escalators, mincing gingerly onto the moving steps in what was a kind of visual metaphor for China's conveyor belt of economic progress. And when the escalator paused momentarily, they stood at the top, unsure whether to follow my lead and walk down the stationary steps instead.

Although Guangzhou's underground train system was expanded to accommodate the 2010 Asian Games, it is already bursting at the seams. At the platform level I joined the thick rush-hour crowd. As the train doors opened, people rushed towards the carriage before the passengers had a chance to disembark, one tide of humanity pushing back the opposing tide. In London, such a scrum would spark outrage, but people here weren't angry – they simply pushed one another aside as if they were parting tree branches on a forest excursion. Competition in most of life is a given here. You must fight for what you want.

Inside the carriage, when seats became available, passengers were shockingly quick on the draw to bag them. I, the undisputed champion of London Underground train seat-grabbing, met my match in the citizens of Guangzhou. Even the older passengers were competitive. What they lacked in speed they made up for in outright shamelessness, lunging with a haste that would be considered indecent anywhere else in the world. Even middle-aged men raced against teenage girls, chivalry be damned.

Tempting as it was to do the same, I couldn't bring myself to 'go native'. When a lady beat me to yet another seat she sat back and looked me straight in the eye without a flicker of guilt. And why not? She was a worthy winner. I resolved to raise my game.

The train's looped handholds dangled by my temples. For the first time in my life I could see above many of the standing passengers' heads, even though I'm only five foot five tall. At the next stop, two six-foot-plus Senegalese-looking men stooped to board the train and made Lilliputians out of all of us.

Passengers texted on their phones, drawing squiggly lines that were converted into Chinese characters via the predictive function. This sea of black-haired heads bowed in concentration was the quintessential twenty-first century resting pose – and the enemy of candid photography.

Back on street level, I walked through the Sanyuanli district where almost every square foot of street was dedicated to commerce. Men demoed toy drones and flashing objects I couldn't identify, and at the international watch market, I ogled a glittering sea of Bulgari, Diesel, Versace and Michael Kors knock-off pieces. 'For lady or man?' sellers asked me, their mouths full of food. They lifted their noodle bowls from the top of the glass display cabinets to show huge watch faces encrusted with diamante.

I finally reached the busy Guangyuanxi Road, the hub of African activity. This was the more Anglophone half of Chocolate City. Almost immediately there was more eye contact, more people saying hello to me and doing so in Nigerian accents. Most of them were of the Igbo ethnic group and therefore of Christian background.

I was among my compatriots.

The smell of Chinese-brand cigarettes and egg waffles thickened the air. Local African residents leaned languidly against the railings while their fellow sub-Saharans – the visiting traders – loaded boxes into taxis with contrasting verve. Two Black men sat on roadside stools getting their shoes shined by Chinese women. Chinese vendors and local policemen shared these streets with Africans, a familiarity that bred a mix of affection and contempt. I would catch one police officer glaring at people, while another cop exchanged smiled greetings and gently stroked the cheek of a Black man as he passed him.

Rickshaws and motorcycle taxis weaved past cheap shop hoardings and people selling corn-on-the-cob from wheel-barrows. Two Chinese men unloaded African yams from a van. One Chinese-run restaurant was unimaginatively named Africa Restaurant, a half-arsed simulacrum containing not much actual African cuisine. The seventies buildings, the Anglophone shop hoardings, the concrete flyover colonised by creeping vines, resembled many a city in Africa. A railway line bisected the street from below.

Nearby stood Canaan Market, where Africans come to buy clothes, shoes and sports apparel. The market was in a large, knackered building; its damp, cavernous air was filled with the screech of adhesive tape being wrapped around cardboard boxes. It was a bazaar of garishness: manning the corridors were white mannequins – fibreglass Vikings modelling kaftans and kufi hats; blue-eyed plastic children wearing faux-gold Africa-shaped pendants and Gucci knock-off T-shirts festooned with the kind of glitter that exfoliates your flesh on contact.

Canaan Market, and Chocolate City as a whole, was a real estate cast-off in itself. The market was built in 1990 as a leather-trading centre, which never took off. Derelict and forlorn, the area became a haven for Chinese drug dealers and was earmarked for demolition, but in 2003 the local authorities decided to designate it as a jeans market for African buyers and sellers. By 2007 the trade by sub-Saharans was worth US$10 million a year and breathed life into the local economy.

Guangzhou's factories clothed a substantial portion of Africa. This was the source of the sub-Saharan textile market collapse. Nigeria banned foreign importation of textiles in 2002, but still they come from China thanks to bribery at customs, undercutting local textile production.

I could see the stalls diagonally opposite Canaan Market, run by friendly Cantonese ladies. The sight of them handling piles of African waxed prints was, to my eyes, as culturally transgressive as those male shop assistants who handle ladies' underwear in Saudi lingerie shops.

Shoes and clothes were spread out on mats on the pavements, going for prices so low they permanently redefined the term 'bargain'. I bought a pair of sliders for US$1.50.

A London-based Nigerian lady told me she was looking

for high-tops for her teenage son but she was worried about buying the wrong trainers. 'He will say I have embarrassed him,' she smiled as she examined the midsole and trimmings. Certain trainers had 'Nkie', not 'Nike', printed on their sides. Some Chinese manufacturers don't care about spelling – they simply like the Roman alphabet because its variety of fonts allows for more artistic expression, unlike Chinese characters.

African buyers haggled with the Chinese for this stuff in a process that could be fraught at times. I witnessed heated face-offs, arms flung skywards in anger, due mainly to cultural differences. In Africa, bartering is an art form, performed with banter and perhaps a smile.

'Nigerian market woman will pet you,' one Nigerian man told me. 'She will tell you why it is costing this much – the trouble with her business . . . The Chinese? They just charge you.'

It was a cross-cultural misunderstanding. Africans assume that a Chinese person's initial asking price is far above the real price, when in actual fact the Chinese don't start particularly high. They cannot understand why Africans ask for prices below the bottom line. The slightest hint of a negotiation sent certain Guangzhou vendors into a rage. '*Mafan!*' they cried. 'Troublesome!'

I got a first-hand taste of this at a shop that sold rucksacks. When I requested a discount for one item, the shopkeeper reacted as if I had just pinched her arse. She was scary looking too: her fringe and pollution mask combined to cover her entire face save for two disgusted eyes. She waved me away with shocking ferocity, her calculator falling from her hand and clattering on the counter. End of discussion. I wasn't even allowed to improve my offer.

I walked on.

There was nothing the Chinese didn't produce and sell, it seemed. Even Nigerian election materials were being manufactured and sold here. Shop windows were plastered with election bunting for Nigeria's two biggest political parties; bracelets proclaiming 'So-and-so 4 Governor'; stickers of election hopefuls like Charles Kenechi Ugwu, whose face tilted righteously above the words: 'The Lord's Chosen . . . Divine gift to Nsukka people'. Rumour has it that the ballot papers for one of Kenya's general elections were delivered to Nairobi from the Chinese printers with Xs already marked in the box for the ruling party.

Next to the election paraphernalia were Nigerian police uniforms and badges on display. To my surprise, the vendor gave me prices on request. At that moment I realised I could clothe my own fake police force if I wanted to (police imposters are a real problem in Nigeria, to the extent that every policeman's name tag now has to be woven into his or her shirt to counter such fraud). One wholesale order – no questions asked – was all I needed to 'establish my authority' on the streets of Lagos or Port Harcourt. Which was as amusing as it was alarming. That the apparel of such a crucial branch of Nigerian governance could be sold so casually in Guangzhou spoke volumes about the power imbalance between China and my mother continent. Across Africa, the Chinese have bought up huge tracts of farmland and mining concessions with the consent of the national leaders, but in China foreigners aren't allowed majority ownership of even the smallest hole-in-the-wall food outlet.

I stepped out onto the street again. A trio of Nigerian 'market women' walked past, wearing boubous and carrying bags of merchandise on their heads. They had curly-mop hair weaves, eyebrows like painted caterpillars, dark lips contrasting ghoulishly against bleached skin. These ladies negotiated the streets of Guangzhou with the blinkered nonchalance of the business traveller. The vision of them sauntering along the road could easily be transposed to their ancestral villages where, like their forebears, they might have trekked several miles to fetch water – a time-consuming task that drains productivity. Instead, they had 'trekked' halfway round the world to Guangzhou. It seemed a long way to go to fetch life's everyday items.

—

'I jealous these people.' Leo shook his head. We were standing further down that same Guangyuanxi Road, surveying the buses, the swept streets and proper sidewalks, free of open drainage. Neon was everywhere, supported by a reliable electricity supply. And yet another McDonald's.

Leo was a tall, middle-aged retailer from Lagos, Nigeria, and was in town to stock up on clothes. I had bumped into him and we proceeded to do what Nigerians always do when in other countries – grumble about Nigeria.

'What this country has and we do not have in our country is quite enormous,' Leo said. 'Anywhere you want to travel in this country you can do that with this train. About five years ago it was not like this here,' he pointed to the built-up shops nearby. 'Even three years ago, it was not like this here. This country has a reserve of, I think, thirty trillion US dollars. Enormous wealth. The US don't even have it.'

We observed our surroundings with a clenched admiration. In the 1950s, Mao Zedong plunged the country into famine with communist agricultural policies under a Cultural Revolution that killed millions and damaged thousands of years of civilisation through state-sponsored destruction of antiquities. Around that time, countries like Nigeria had hopes for a bright future, and Africans studying in China in the 1960s sniffed at the drop in living standards. How the tables have turned.

Leo stayed in Guangzhou for a month at a time, communicating with wholesalers in 'commercial Chinese' ('how much', 'what colour', 'which size'). He shared twenty- or forty-foot shipping containers with other established Nigerian business owners. This was not a game for novices. Buying products that are so subject to personal taste and faddism did not pose a personal risk for Leo. He had his ear on the ground, a close relationship with his customer base. Unlike large-scale Western buyers, African buyers don't dictate fashions – they satisfy their customers' expressed wishes, meaning that Leo rarely suffered dead inventory, which is the scourge of big buyers. Everything gets shifted eventually.

It costs at least £5,000 to fly to Guangzhou, fill a container with goods and ship it back to the UK or Nigeria. Providing the exporter sold all their merchandise and their currency behaved itself against the dollar, they would make a profit. It seemed a pity that Leo should come this far for cheap clothes when Nigeria once had its own textile industry.

'Why can the Chinese do this and Nigerians won't?' I asked.

'This country, they love their country,' he said. 'They are very resilient, very hardworking. They want to improve their country. They want to do everything to make sure that their country moves forward. Our country, we don't love our country. People at the head, they loot the fund of you and me and put it in their pocket. Somebody who is doing that . . . is that person patriotic? Never. He never loves his country. He only loves himself. Wants to feed himself only. But here, if they ever find you in corruption at whatever level, you're going to be jailed. Even your relations who enjoyed that money. So they don't ever, ever encourage corruption. It is not common here the way it is in Nigeria.' Leo kissed his teeth. 'It's a very big shame.'

Leo was being too kind to China. Corruption *is* a problem here, but it doesn't cannibalise the national infrastructure to the extent that it does in Nigeria. Chinese-American China specialist Minxin Pei reckons Chinese kickbacks, bribery, theft and waste of public funds account for 3 per cent of GDP. President Xi Jinping dishes out punishment for corruption, though it tends to be to provincial and local-level minions rather than those in the top tier. Between 2013 and 2016, about one million officials were punished for bribery, abuse of power or incompetence. A few of those were top ministers, although some critics claim these punishments were the premier's way of eliminating his rivals, a purge masquerading as virtue. In 2022, China punished more than 600,000 officials for 'violating Communist Party discipline and laws,' the majority of them being lower-level officials in farming communities. Only thirty-six higher-level provincial party cadres and cabinet-level officials were involved in misconduct cases.

Then there is the concept of *guanxi*, a fundamental feature of Chinese culture. It's a system that emphasises obligations and reciprocity between people, and is built over time through social exchanges and mutual favours. By establishing this type of relationship with someone, the other party is implicitly agreeing to reciprocate when the need arises. It goes without saying that, in a political or corporate context, the line between guanxi and corruption becomes blurred.

I parted ways with Leo and continued down the street, past a sex shop and the nail salons. Sanyuanli's pavements were lightly littered with calling cards of cargo handlers and companies that teach 'business Chinese' to African clients. These displayed stock Chinese phrases that clothing manufacturers would use on their African clients:

'This price is only for the old friend'
'We have a factory there is no middle man'
'Quality is as good as the original goods'

Missing from this list are phrases such as 'You are cheating me', or 'I want my money back', or 'This is not the merchandise I requested', or 'You said you would deliver it in one week, not two!' Such phrases would have come in handy for the Ghanaian lady I saw in the lobby of the Tongtong hotel further along the Guangyuanxi Road. Standing in front of a mountain of Ghana Must Go bags, she wore an elegant African print dress and looked supremely pissed off.

'They told me the things will be ready,' she grumbled in a gravelly voice. 'Now they are saying two more weeks!'

It was a common story, wholesalers misleading customers about availability. Akua now had to spend an extra fortnight's hotel accommodation in Guangzhou. This was one of the reasons people overstayed their visas. One month is not enough to check merchandise, visit factories, deal with shipping agents and complete one's business transaction.

—

I moved to a hotel in the Haizhu district towards the southern end of the city centre. The receptionist took down my passport details and searched for my visa as if he were an airport immigration official. To his left was a bank of screens, monitoring activities around the hotel. From where I was standing some of the images looked like bedrooms. Perhaps wholesale surveillance of citizens was so normalised it extended to hotels? Would there be hidden cameras in my room too? I decided to throw caution to the wind; at the price offered the room was too good to turn down, hidden cameras or not. In the bathroom, my toilet had an Apple logo for a flush, which was either a mindless piece of decoration, or a big fuck you to US intellectual property laws. Either way it brightened up my day.

The next morning I decided to explore other parts of Guangzhou, beyond Sanyuanli. I walked through the Ximenkou and Haizhu districts, along streets that were covered by overhanging buildings, designed to protect the pavements from monsoon rains. From the main roads' advertising billboards, male models stared down at me. They were big-eyed and square-jawed, and their female counterparts wore white foundation and European-pink blusher which clashed with their jet-black hair. Even in the twenty-first century, the parasol skin tones of housebound aristocrats are still considered more attractive than the paddy peasant suntan.

I grew to love Haizhu Nanzhou Street. Life here hummed agreeably. I walked along porticos occupied by hair salons, metal workshops, bakeries, fishmongers and small hardware stores. One guy crafted dragon costumes for the New Year celebrations. In nail salons, chunky macho men redefined masculinity by dragging on cigarettes while receiving pedicures. And in between the modernity, the old world still operated within it like an interlocking universe: men pushed wheeled goods carts against the flow of traffic, and nearly collided with dawdling pedestrians who gazed at their smartphones without looking where they were going.

Life is lived out on the street. An old man sat on a chair on the pavement reading a newspaper; a little further down another person snoozed on an armchair that had been plonked out in the open air. The residents were neither poor nor rich; they enjoyed smartphones and other trappings of the post-industrial world, yet they maintained an old-school, small-enterprise simplicity – it was that perfect sweet spot on the economic maturity curve where mid-stage industrial development intersected with the Information Age.

—

Forty years previously, while Nigeria was urbanising, this Guangzhou neighbourhood comprised several agricultural villages where farmers grazed water buffalo, not far from Zhonshan University campus. In 1979 the streetlights were so few and far between that Richard L. Williams described how car headlights were often the only source of illumination and that cyclists would suddenly loom up 'just a couple of feet in front'. It was hard to comprehend the extent and speed of change that had taken place here within my lifetime.

People's reactions to me as a Black person varied. My appearance defied categorisation. My short Afro hairstyle distinguished me from the African female prostitutes who generally wore hair weaves. And the DSLR camera I carried added an extra layer of differentiation. Being British as well as Nigerian, I entered certain spaces – the type that many Africans didn't frequent – with the casual entitlement of the Western tourist.

Guangzhou folk were playful and irreverent and far friendlier than I'd anticipated. In a small park east of Ximenkou, groups of middle-aged men and women played foot shuttlecock with impressive skill. One trio motioned for me to join them. I was dying to have a go (I had never tried it before) but I didn't want to disrupt their flow, so I declined and watched. As far back as the Song dynasty, the elderly have been encouraged to do exercise and cultivate their brains. China has long been ahead of the game in understanding how to keep body and mind healthy. In the modern age, this ethos created a scenario in which the older generation were the ones busying themselves with physical, outdoor activities while the youngsters were sedentary, heads bent over phones or laptop screens.

Dog walkers smiled as they passed me. Others, usually the more rural ones, giggled when they saw me approaching. A small minority glared.

Some customers' behaviour at lunch had me in for a culture shock. I was in a mid-market restaurant, the type that had uniformed waiters and waitresses and tablecloths. A well-dressed, three-generation family sat to my left. To my right were an ageing couple, fresh from the countryside and shabbily attired. The woman's hands and fingernails were flecked with black dirt. Her husband was a mess, and maintained the demeanour of a man ground down by either poverty or decades of his wife's incontinent chatter. He grunted and nodded intermittently as she screeched like a cat trapped in a house blaze. When the woman caught sight of me she swivelled round to ogle, one arm slung casually over the back of her chair, the other hand clutching a piece of meat, her mouth chewing. The intensity of her gaze, the lack of inhibition, the brazenness of it – and from such close range – made my blood boil. My return glare didn't deter her. It only invited her to start talking to me. Her tone sounded harsh. Was she angry, mocking, friendly or just ill? I couldn't tell. Then her husband leaned to the side of the table, hawked up phlegm and spat it on the floor.

I dropped my chopsticks and slammed my palms against my ears, a reflex reaction that always came too late. A waitress caught my eye and chuckled in sympathy. I soldiered on with my meal, trying to ignore the old lady and the pool of phlegm on the floor but my appetite was dead and gone. I got up and left.

My parents visited China in the very early 1980s. My mother told me that on domestic flights each seat came with a spittoon attached. It was the longest flight of her life. But the glorious thing about China is its willingness and ability to change age-old habits when necessary. When the world descended on Beijing for the 2008 Olympic Games, citizens were banned from spitting during that fortnight, and police blasted loud horns in the face of anyone caught in the act. Perhaps as a result of this, people under the age of thirty hardly spit any more. It was usually men above a certain age who I could count on to fire bullets of snot towards my feet, but these were fewer and farther between than they might have been in the past, which was a relief.

They had some way to go in terms of gender recognition, however. Visits to public toilets became a fraught issue for me thanks to my short hair. The toilet attendants often had trouble recognising that I was female, and they would stop me and gesticulate at the gender sign on the door until they either realised their mistake or a colleague assured them it was OK.

One cleaner was particularly strident in her gender blindness. It happened one evening in a semi-dark public toilet next to a park. On entering a cubicle I heard the urgent screeches of an elderly lady behind me. I held the door ajar as the bent frame of the cleaner hurried stiffly in my direction. Without understanding any Chinese I knew what the lady was saying. Trying to contain my bladder, I stepped forward into the light to give her a clearer view of my earrings, my lipstick and curvy hips. It made no difference. She continued gesticulating that I was in the wrong toilets.

'I'm a woman,' I told her in English. The androgynous timbre of my voice obviously didn't help matters. There was only one thing to do: I unzipped my top, ran my palms down my chest and stuck out my boobs.

Satisfied, the cleaner waved me on to pee in peace.

—

Visa overstayers weren't hard to find; they were hidden in plain sight around Sanyuanli. In need of a haircut, I scoured the streets in search of a barber. There was a marked contrast between the body language of African business visitors and the Africans who lived permanently in Guangzhou. The former moved purposefully and hastily and were of mixed gender. The latter were almost all men – languid and largely young. They leaned against the street railings near the McDonald's opposite Canaan Market, chatting, greeting passing friends and seemingly doing nothing. I approached a group, all of them Igbo, to ask where I could get a haircut. A guy with short hair twists stood up, unfolded his arms and signalled for me to follow him.

'You're a barber?' I asked.

He nodded.

I'd hit the bullseye on only my second attempt.

That's how things work among the community here. No signs, no open-air advertisements or solicitations, just a tacit provision of services based on informal networks.

The man, 'Saul', led me down to the windowless basement of a small shopping complex, through a forest of cheap clothes and shoes and into a minuscule room. For some reason he glanced furtively down the corridor before closing the concertina door and picking up his scissors. Dialogue with Saul was near impossible. Taciturn, grinning, monosyllabic, evasive – all I could prise out of him was that he was studying at a university in Yunnan Province and that haircutting was his side hustle while visiting Guangzhou to see his brother, Promise.

Promise was a lot chattier. I sat with him and some others, including Emmanuel, a Nigerian, and a Filipina called Bea.

Bea had spent five years in Hong Kong, then lived in Macao, and was now in Guangzhou until she was ready to move on. Her age was indeterminate, the motivation behind her peripatetic life a mystery she wasn't prepared to reveal.

We sat on plastic stools in the corridor, between a forest of cheap, shiny clothes and a hair and beauty shop. Customers were few on the ground. Food smells emanated from a restaurant in the back, and a striking-looking Chinese woman ferried boxes of jollof rice and other African dishes to customers within the building. She was unconventional in every sense. Dressed in black leather trousers and leather cap, she stood almost six feet tall in her stiletto boots as she strode briskly about the place. Her olive suntan was a rebellion in itself, flying in the face of the pallid tone desired by wider society. She was magnificent.

Promise was cuddling his friend's baby, a cute little mixed-race girl called Chioma. Her Chinese mother was so quiet I couldn't tell whether she spoke English or not. She sat in her nearby shop, packing boxes of hair extensions and African beauty products for export.

I turned to chat with Emmanuel, another Igbo man. A low Afro haircut fringed his face. His eyes were beautiful, obsidian, and they regarded me with an amicable interest that turned to suspicion as I asked question after question. Emmanuel had studied computer engineering and fibre optics at university in Nigeria but stayed jobless three years after graduating. 'Female students got jobs more easily . . . they give something for something,' he said. Emmanuel moved to China to play professional football, until injury forced him to retire. Eight years on he couldn't face returning to Nigeria; so haunted was he by his postgraduate unemployment there he would rather take his chances in China on an expired visa.

Now he spent his days sitting outside this clothes stall, nursing a slight paunch. His shop was a tiny nine-foot-square indent. He hung a couple of football T-shirts on the wall to give the illusion of a sports apparel outlet, but his real job was selling VPNs (virtual private networks that allow users to bypass China's firewall, which blocks access to Google and Facebook).

How did Emmanuel like China?

'Chinese are the opposite to human beings,' Emmanuel said, his voice calm and low. 'The man stamping your passport may be having trouble with his girlfriend. And because he is angry he will transfer his vexation onto you. He will not give you visa. And when they give you visa they take joy in charging you more.'

The government visa policy had toughened up. New rules gave immigration officials free rein to deny foreigners visas or entry into China without having to give an explanation for their decision. Inevitably Africans were targeted, their high-viz skin marking them out above the white Europeans and Arabs who regularly overstayed their visas too. In 2008, the authorities launched a heavy crackdown on sub-Saharan visa overstayers ahead of the Beijing Olympics. Those who gave themselves up to the police had to pay a 10,000 yuan fine, otherwise they were detained for three to four months before being deported and banned from China for five years.

For Nigerians, the days of three-month visas were long gone. Now they were only allocated thirty days. Renewing them involved buying a train or bus ticket to Hong Kong or Macao, then paying £100 for a visa. Every month. The expense was too much for Emmanuel, so he stayed on the mainland on an expired visa. Not that proper documentation would get him a job – China doesn't need unskilled, semi-skilled or even skilled workers. If anything, China was exporting its excess labour to Africa.

Guys like Emmanuel made up a significant chunk of the African population in Guangzhou. Verifying their numbers was, and remains, impossible. They survive by providing services to other immigrants. Every waking hour is spent avoiding the police who occasionally sweep through the Sanyuanli shopping complexes on visa raids. Laying low during the day, Emmanuel and the others come out at night, in synch with cockroaches and other nocturnal creatures.

Even when their finances permit it, moving around China is also difficult for people in Emmanuel's situation. Forget trains or planes – passport ID is mandatory for those forms of transport. With the government eyeballing the move-ments of citizens and immigrants alike, achingly long bus journeys are the only way for visa overstayers to traverse this vast country.

Emmanuel and his friends' days were confined to the basement of this shopping centre. It was a claustrophobic place, and after a couple of hours I grew tired of its harsh artificial lighting. It was from this limited perspective – and from the internet – that Emmanuel based his opinions on Chinese people and society.

'They eat human foetuses,' he told me.

'Whaaat?'

He and Bea nodded authoritatively in the affirmative.

The Chinese, they claimed, had no souls, no morals, no boundaries.

'You can see it on Weibo,' Bea informed me, referring to the Chinese social media website. She would show me the footage 'another time'.

Didn't all mammalian embryos kind of look alike? No, Emmanuel insisted, it was definitely human.

I was sceptical. Already I could see that Chinese and Africans were observing one another through the distorting prism of the internet, which was ripe for misinterpretation and validated prejudices. There was no context, no easy way to separate truth from spoof. My Google searches yielded mobile phone footage of brawls between Black and Chinese men with no indication of how such incidents started. Who were the villains and heroes? Viewers are free to project biases and assumptions.

Seen through curated cyberspace, China can seem incomprehensible. The former tabloid website *Shanghaiist* posted sensational videos which, though not necessarily insightful, were hilarious or shocking, and they encompassed the full spectrum of behaviour one would expect from a country that contains one fifth of all humanity. Anyone looking for displays of genius, stupidity, cruelty or kindness will find it in this eccentric and diverse nation. There's the heart-warming story of the old man who adopted six children, raised them single-handedly, and was reunited with his middle-aged brood to celebrate his ninety-sixth birthday. Then there was the psycho lorry driver who, for reasons unknown, took exception to the automobile ahead of him and shunted the tiny vehicle from behind. The terrified driver of the car scrambled out and sprinted away, but the truck carried on chasing after him. It mounted the pavement and crashed through the central reservation in mindless, dogged pursuit.

There was also the photo of school children being forced to sit in an outdoor classroom while swathed in smog so dense they could barely see their own hands; or the woman who rested her bare feet on a table at Starbucks, then spat at the employee who asked her to desist. Was she suffering from mental ill-health or just being obnoxious? The viewer doesn't know.

My favourite was the story of two ladies who argued on the street for eight hours straight on a hot summer's day, the argument ending only when both of them fainted. Almost as good was the story about the truck driver who reversed his vehicle for a full kilometre after missing his highway exit. Then there was the woman who attacked her husband's mistress with scissors, shredding her clothes and her hair in full view of the public.

With half a billion smartphones in the country, there was always an amateur camera crew on standby to record any craziness.

Visa overstayers like Emmanuel experienced Chinese society through this internet lens. Likewise, the Chinese people saw Nigerians like Emmanuel through whatever footage their internet was feeding them, the two sides interacting in person mainly through financial transactions, which were often fraught.

'Would you prefer to live in Nigeria?' I asked Emmanuel.

He nodded. 'The Chinese, they don't have human rights. The government tells them what to do. They don't have freedom.'

Emmanuel spent his days beneath the glare of these artificial lights, garrisoned by clothes racks in this subterranean space, ever poised to flee from the police. He could have been king of his homeland shack, but instead he became a prisoner in a foreign castle.

The reason someone like Emmanuel might leave home for a life abroad that is not much better was perfectly summarised by the late Kenyan writer Binyavanga Wainaina in one of his Facebook status updates:

> It's not that he becomes rich, even if he's living on the streets and it's cold and horrible in Barcelona – he comes home and he can marry. You have 34-year-olds who can't marry and are staying in their parents' home. People are like: 'I can rather live in hell. I would rather eat chicken shit across the Sahara. Because I am a person with hunger, desire, to control the world in my own terms.'

Stasis, dynamism, agency and restriction – how we define these states of being is a matter of personal interpretation.

—

I wanted to know what kind of apartments Africans lived in. The enquiry was partly for my own benefit as I was itching to move out of hotel accommodation to cut down on my costs. What did working-class accommodation look like in China?

Promise (brother of Saul the barber) told me I could rent a decent place for £65 a month. He introduced me to Mary, a housing agent whose tiny office was tucked between two Nigerian clothes stalls upstairs. Mary was Chinese, in her fifties, bespectacled, with an elegant bob and razor-sharp fringe. Familiar with African immigrants and focused on money-making, she received me unquestioningly, her eyes barely processing my presence.

'At 9 p.m. we go see apartment.' Her heavily accented pidgin English was just about intelligible.

That evening, we mounted motorcycle taxis in the pouring rain, Mary on one bike, Promise and me sharing the second. Promise told me the name of the neighbourhood. It was a vague, disyllabic word. He couldn't tell me its location in the city because he didn't use maps. Nor could he tell me how to spell it in pinyin, the romanised Chinese script. There was no way of bridging the gap between Chinese phonetics and my Google map. I was heading into the night towards some mystery district.

We toured various '70s mid-rise tower blocks. They were dark and grey, separated by low-lit alleyways. A giant puddle reflected the street lighting, which rippled beneath the footsteps of a rat. The one-bedroom apartments – all Formica floors and spine-bending mattresses – were occupied largely by single African men. I thought I wasn't above staying in such a place for a month or two, but that was before I spotted the squat toilet. A hole in the floor. No way was I offloading into that. Western-style crappers may be less hygienic on some level but I'm accustomed to them. I'm a queen who needs to sit on a throne. 'I'll think about it,' I lied to Mary before we parted ways.

After Mary returned home, Promise offered to show me his living quarters across town. We hailed a taxi. On his phone he showed me video footage of him hanging out with his friend, a Nigerian footballer who played for Guangzhou's Evergrande Taobao professional football club. The pair of them were in the footballer's smart apartment, socialising with other guests, including the Nigerian rapper Ruggedman. Promise looked like he was enjoying his life in this city.

We arrived at the hotel he lived in. The place was run by two friendly and corpulent Chinese women who had hung a bilingual sign on the wall that said, 'Do Not Gob Here'. We walked up the stairs and along the first-floor corridor. A few of the doors were ajar, giving me glimpses of African male tenants, each of them solitary long-term residents in these glorified dormitories. Was Promise OK with this living arrangement? He nodded indifferently. Countless global migrant communities around the world have begun in male dormitories and hotels like this. They're supposed to be a means to an end – but to what end? Did all this compromise and hardship – 'eating bitter' as they say in China – ever have a sweet aftertaste for these Africans? It felt like a dissonance that would never resolve.

I was examining the bathroom when I heard the door close. Promise walked towards me and pointed to a beer on the table. 'Want a drink?' It was close to 11 p.m. and there was nowhere to sit except his bed. Suddenly it occurred to me he might be steering our evening towards a 'happy ending'. Maybe I was imagining things. But if not, I couldn't blame him for making the assumption. He didn't know I was a writer, and most women wouldn't ask to see a man's living quarters for platonic reasons.

'Sorry, I have to go,' I told him, and made my way out.

II

DREAM BIG

Sunday. One would never have guessed it, there was so much noise and bustle, not a hint of slowing down. In China, the Judeo-Christian Sabbath is considered a needless disruption of productivity. For the Africans, though, I knew Sunday was worship day. I was hoping it would be a good place to find Africans to talk to – the middle-class, non-illegal kind. I wanted to find out more about being Christian in a communist country like China. Abrahamic religions here are low in visibility and intensity, coming a distant fifth and sixth behind Buddhism, money and smartphones.

It was a bitterly cold and sleety afternoon, with temperatures plummeting to one degree thanks to an unusual weather front sweeping across eastern Asia. The Arctic blast had killed sixty people already and I was in danger of becoming casualty number sixty-one. Teeth chattering, and dangerously underdressed, I battled the crowded Yide Road south of the city, close to the Pearl River. Beneath Yide Road's porticos were spice markets and a shop where shark fins were displayed individually in glass jars, like Damien Hirst art exhibits. A man offered me bundles of seaweed that looked exactly like straightened Afro hair but tasted mildly better. He wiggled his hips to convey its medicinal benefits (loose translation: good for the joints but impairs your rhythm dancing).

Suddenly, the busy market portico stopped and gave out onto a spacious square and the twin spires of a European Gothic Revival church. I had gone from the Orient to municipal France in a matter of seconds. The Shishi Catholic church (Sacred Heart Cathedral) stood at the southern end of the square. Built in 1860 during the Second Empire with financial backing from Napoleon III, the cathedral was initially frequented by Europeans. The French obtained the site from the Qing dynasty emperor as compensation after French property was destroyed during the first Opium War. Now the congregation was mainly African.

Christianity and China go back a long way (China had a bishop before Britain ever did) but the relationship has a fraught history. While Christianity and Islam spread easily in areas of the world where literacy was non-existent or nascent, both religions hit the buffers on Chinese civilisation. The Christian missionaries who managed to penetrate the Middle Kingdom were brought by merchants rather than the state, which meant they were more willing to concede to the demands of Chinese rulers.

Those rulers weren't interested in Jesus, but they did take a liking to some of the ideas and innovations connected to Christianity, such as Western painting techniques, brought to them by Giuseppe Castiglione, an Italian Jesuit painter. Castiglione introduced Western perspective projection (in which objects in the distance look smaller) as opposed to the Chinese axonometric projection in which background objects are piled up vertically. The Qing dynasty court lapped it up but still gave New Testament scripture a wide berth.

By the mid-nineteenth century Christianity had negative connotations in China, exacerbated by defeat at the hands of the British during the Opium Wars. In the twentieth century, as this distrust faded, its potential influence was suppressed, successive governments following Chairman Mao's lead in banning proselytisation.

Protestantism is experiencing a modern revival in China, but adherents are still a minority (a whopping 100 million, but a minority nonetheless), often running underground missionary operations. Christians are allowed to worship, albeit strictly behind closed doors – no street-corner preaching or attempts at recruitment – and their churches, such as this Shishi church, are controlled by the Communist Party.

China has been known to deport African pastors who dare to proselytise or carry out missionary activities on its soil – Senior Pastor of the Royal Victory Church Daniel Enyeribe Michael was expelled from China for openly confronting Chinese officials concerning religious freedom – so how do African Christians, so loud and keen to spread the 'Good News', practise their faith under such restrictions?

I hoped to find out at this church in Guangzhou. I stood shivering outside its granite exterior. In the eyes of Guangzhou residents, the Shishi church was an aesthetic curiosity, a little corner of Europe deposited near the Pearl River and, more importantly, a cool backdrop for selfies. In the church court-yard, Chinese tourists flicked V 'peace' signs and posed with a man in a monkey costume that smelled like it hadn't been washed since the year of the monkey in 1968. A motley crew of crippled and disfigured Chinese beggars clustered at the gate, stretching out their hands to African churchgoers who swept past them and took seats inside. A Chinese priest in a black gown and mustard socks paced the grounds on a phone call. If someone had told me as a child that I and other Africans would be attending a Catholic church service in communist China at a French cathedral with a man in a monkey suit standing outside, I would have thought I was hallucinating.

I walked inside. Soaring granite walls, huge stained-glass windows. Filipinos in church gowns wielded tithe offering bags. The congregation was predominantly Nigerian and Congolese and male, with a smattering of Afro-Chinese families. I shivered in the wintry air and covered my head with the hood of my coat. The church's organ was destroyed during the Cultural Revolution (when Mao ordered the destruction of antiquities and temples in order to instil communist values) and was replaced by an old piano that couldn't do justice to the building's grand acoustics. That, and the accented singing, produced an incongruously African village sound.

Sitting in the wooden pews were groups of young Chinese cultural voyeurs, rucksacks still on their backs. Their intrigued eyes took in the high ceilings and stained-glass images of burning bushes and other Old Testament themes. When they weren't giggling and whispering they were fiddling with their phones, to the irritation of the Nigerian church volunteer who patrolled the aisles like a scowling schoolmaster. He ordered them to remove their feet from the prayer cushions and switch off their phones. He motioned me to take down my jacket hood. There was a dress code here. I had seen it on the China Travel website: 'Short skirts, knickers and slippers are not allowed in the cathedral,' it said. (The knickers ban was presumably a typo – no way was I exposing my 'undercarriage' in this winter chill).

While the Chinese priest delivered the service in English, groups of onlookers shuffled in and out, lending an air of permanent restlessness. It felt like karma for every Chinese temple invaded by Western tourists.

At the end of the service, as the church emptied, I approached the stern volunteer for conversation. He was Pastor David, a Nigerian, who broke into a surprisingly lovely smile. 'Ninety per cent of Africans here are Nigerian –' he began, before a Chinese lady interrupted him to complain in Mandarin that her bag had been stolen during the service.

'It is these Chinese thieves,' the pastor explained to me. 'They don't come here to serve God. They will take your things when you are not looking. You will be praying and they just take it.' That's why he patrolled the aisles. Anyway, the pastor couldn't chat for too long, he needed to prepare for a charismatic Pentecostal prayer service, which was about to begin in the building next door.

I followed him there.

—

The charismatic service was everything the Catholic service was not: raucous and fervent, with a four-piece band playing music amped up through huge speakers that dwarfed the hall and forced me to cover my ears. The room had the familiar charismatic look: bunting hanging from the ceiling, and a sea of white plastic chairs – the kind that get shunted around during bursts of rapture.

'With God nothing is impossible!' the pastor (not David) boomed down the mike. The congregation – overwhelmingly male – responded with cheers so deep and loud we could've been in a boxing arena.

The few Chinese people present were all women – wives and girlfriends, lifelong Christians who, to my surprise, had not converted on account of their Nigerian menfolk (and even if they had, the government was more concerned about Chinese men and their families becoming Christians). The women sat with their fidgety, mixed-race kids in a corner. One lady clamped her naughty daughter between her knees and smacked the girl repeatedly, accompanying each wallop with staccato bursts of Cantonese. I had tried striking up conversation with these women ('What's it like being Christian and Chinese?') before the service started, but they were tight-lipped. With glazed eyes, their children watched the pastor pace the stage and preach about wealth and prosperity. He was quoting bits of the Bible relating to miracles or transformation of one's destiny. Such talk was apt in this context, since it really did take a miracle for Africans to get rich within China's iron fist. 'If you have been hustling for twenty years in China and you have nothing to show for it,' he roared, 'then something is wrong!'

The pastor disparaged those Nigerians who repatriate themselves over Christmas only to be contaminated by 'occultic vampires'. Those who spent time 'watching Manchester United Champions League football instead of praying must be spiritually fortified,' he barked.

Sometimes the pastor spoke in tongues; other times he sprinkled his sermon with Igbo. A constant in his theme was the immigrants' desire to impress their doubters – especially the Chinese in-laws – and prove that their move to China had been worthwhile. The pastor painted an imaginary scenario: 'Your Chinese father-in-law is criticising you for driving a second-hand car,' he growled. 'But the spirit of God will lead you to a greener pasture.' Prayer, combined with hard work, could solve that problem, he said. Then he mimed turning up at the father-in-law's house years later, waving imaginary keys to an expensive car. 'Where are you now?' he grinned triumphantly. The congregation roared their appreciation. 'You cannot be in the presence of God and you will be barren. Dream big!'

Everyone shouted the mantra over and over again. 'Dream big!' My neighbour turned to me, patted my thigh and smiled, 'Dream big.'

Pastor: 'You will prosper in this, the land of China. You will take control of the Chinese economy!'

Congregants moved around the room, shaking hands with one another and murmuring a mantra that alluded to John 4:10 – 'I am in the presence of the Lord therefore I cannot be dry.' Sitting this one out might've looked churlish, so I joined in. This exercise marked the end of the service, I assumed. Turns out I was wrong. The pastor went on and on and on (three hours and ticking), and my yawns grew more frequent. At one point I woke up with my mouth gaping at the ceiling.

For privacy, I retreated to the back of the hall. Standing in the back row were two middle-aged Chinese women and a man, gawping at the spectacle. Judging by their shabby clothes and wrinkled suntans they were fresh from the countryside. The trio's bemusement teetered on amusement. Most curious was the grey-haired man whose head twitched in all directions as he examined our African faces.

Had I been able to speak Chinese I would have explained

to him that these African worshippers were combining spiritual worship with money. Being Chinese, he probably would've understood perfectly. His people's beliefs are governed by spiritual forces to some extent, but underpinned by a financial pragmatism and a love of money that Nigerian Pentecostalism shares – two cultures with similar outlooks, yet manifested so differently.

By 7 p.m. the service still hadn't finished. I had planned on staying until the end so I could chat to people but I was starving, so I left.

—

I thought about those mixed-race children at the church, the Christian Chinese women and their African husbands of similar faith. It made for an interesting and unexpectedly compatible coupling. Since an overwhelming majority of African residents in Guangzhou were men, intermarriage with the Chinese was inevitable.

Chukwu was a perfect example. I first met him in Sanyuanli, above a parade of shops selling commodities for African exporters. I had been absolutely starving but couldn't think of where to eat in such unfamiliar surroundings. Paralysed with indecision and crazed with hunger, I caved in to the Golden Arches. McDonald's was popular with Chinese and Africans, one of the few eateries where both races mixed. (As the singer Boy George once said: 'There's nothing like bad taste to unite the masses.')

As I stood in the queue I saw a shoe shop in the shabby mall on the other side of the glass wall. Inside it, two Chinese women fussed over a half-Black baby, a gorgeous bundle of loose black curls and slightly epicanthic eyes, dark and wide like a seal pup's. After finishing my meal I walked over to them.

They were young, independent-spirited and wore fur-trimmed coats, exuding the strong-mindedness one would expect from women who would choose to cross the racial divide. Neither woman spoke fluent English. One of them, Ma, was dating a skinny Nigerian man standing nearby called Chukwu, with whom she had a three-year-old daughter.

How did Chukwu and Ma meet?

'Over there,' Chukwu smiled. 'In that seat.' He pointed through the glass window to the McDonald's counter. Chukwu had boldly approached Ma and started a 'conversation,' although neither of them spoke the other's language at the time. I guess their bodies did the talking.

Ma and Chukwu had recently taken their daughter on a visit to Nigeria. Ma played me a mobile phone recording of the child saying a few words in her father's Igbo tongue. None of the Nigerians speak to their kids in Igbo much. English and Cantonese were the lingua francas. With the Igbo grandparents being absent and the Chinese grandparents handling much of the childcare, the kids end up fluent in Chinese. However, Ma said she could cook Nigerian dishes like gari and egusi soup, although 'it does not taste as good as his.'

Such unions were happening more and more in Guangzhou. In the racial hierarchy of suitable marriage partners, Africans were not high on most Chinese parents' lists. The Chinese are class conscious, and the rural to urban fault line is deep and civilisational. Some urbanites consider rural migrants little more than shit on one's shoe (and equally infragrant

– smell features heavily in such matters). Still, country folk are legally entitled to own or rent businesses and premises while Africans, and all foreigners, can only own 49 per cent, so African entrepreneurs often arranged for their Chinese wives and girlfriends to front their businesses as the official proprietors. For rural Chinese women like Lin, marrying a 'foreign devil' represented a step up, a chance to own an enterprise she otherwise couldn't afford. It was a win-win situation for both parties. But such conveniences were often, from what I could see, only side-benefits of genuinely romantic unions.

Naturally, when I asked African men why their Chinese wives married them and not a Chinese man, I was given a different theory. I heard all sorts of amusing reasons, such as Chinese men 'not working as hard as the women' or 'Chinese men eat too much sugar so they are less potent in the bedroom'.

Ironically, the rise in interracial marriages owed itself partly to Guangdong Province's crackdown on law-breaking foreigners (known as *sanfei*). The campaign was designed to marginalise them and make their existence in China more precarious. Visa renewals became difficult or impossible, yet it had the effect of driving undocumented Africans even deeper into Chinese society as they ended up marrying Chinese women to get around the visa problem, learning the Chinese language and doing business with locals on the down-low.

—

The jewellery store where Ma, Chukwu and their friends stood was a popular social gathering point. It was there that

I first encountered a Chinese person speaking more than transactional pidgin English. This lady was fluent, and her pronunciation and intonation were almost perfect save for a slight Chinese inflection: 'Zero tharee,' she said as she negotiated the price of a necklace. 'Tharee' was the Nigerian pronunciation of 'three', which is drawn out and disyllabic. The lady jokingly dismissed another necklace that was offered to her. 'I don' want dis one, *jare*. I don't want, o!'

She was bantering with the shop owner, a man called Ikem. Laid out beneath his glass counter were crucifixes the size of mobile phones, silver necklace pendants that formed the word 'MORE', and suchlike. His clientele were mainly African.

When I asked Ikem whether he was Nigerian, his bulbous, blocky features fell as if he had been possessed: 'I am . . . Biafran.'

He was referring to Biafra, the ethnic Igbo 'republic' that tried unsuccessfully to secede from Nigeria in the 1960s. It sparked a civil war from 1967–71 that killed one million people before the Igbo finally surrendered. The episode has been a sore point ever since. Other Nigerians questioned Igbos' allegiance to the country and subsequently froze them out of sections of the economy and politics. The Igbo learned to become financially independent and earned a reputation as skilled entrepreneurs. Their working classes place strong emphasis on apprenticeships for boys, who are sent to work at a friend or relative's shop for years, learning the ropes. The trading opportunities that arose in China have suited these established practices perfectly.

Although it was suppressed in its original iteration, in recent years the Biafran movement, like many nationalist movements around the world, has enjoyed a minor resurgence thanks to social media.

'I'm Biafran,' Ikem repeated. His longed-for republic of Biafra comprised all of south-eastern Nigeria, including non-Igbo ethnic groups such as mine, the Ogoni. We want no part in this secession, and I told Ikem as such.

'We are all Biafrans,' he insisted in presidential tones, his eyes boring through me, his soul transported to a place where logic could not follow. Behind him was a computer monitor broadcasting an old CBS *60 Minutes* documentary on the Biafran civil war. It showed emaciated Biafran children.

Ikem had previously lived in Lagos where he sold imported car engine filters from China until he went bankrupt. When a good friend of his also went bankrupt and moved to China, Ikem followed suit. It was 2003 and he was twenty-eight years old. Ikem stayed at his friend's house here in Guangzhou for a month before getting his own apartment. Six years later he launched his jewellery business. He didn't tell me how he sustained himself financially during those intervening years.

By all appearances, life in China was going well for Ikem. He had a Chinese wife, two young children, a job, a home. Bankruptcy was a distant memory. Yet he felt trapped, implacably so. Years in Guangzhou had made him even more Biafran than the Biafrans back home. His disdain for Nigeria had fermented and calcified out here, and now bordered on an obsession.

'No sane person will stay in Nigeria,' he said. 'They would rather live in Syria or Afghanistan than stay in Nigeria. We Igbo really don't have a home. I see myself as being stateless. And that's the truth. I'm a Biafran. I am in bondage, I'm in prison.'

Didn't life in China suffice?

'I don't belong here. I have a place I should call my home. Because it's not free I have to make it free and call it my home.'

'Even if you have a wife and family here?'

Ikem leaned towards me, across his glass-topped table. 'Every day you are being reminded of where you come from. You have a visa policy that reminds you that you have foreigner status.'

Someone like Ikem, who is married to a Chinese person, is entitled to a permanent residency visa but, bizarrely, it must be renewed every year, even though his children are Chinese citizens. Anyone overstaying their visa is deported and cannot return to China for five years.

'You have day-to-day meetings with locals and possibly with the authorities. Sometimes they come and knock on your door when you're sleeping, when you're eating with your children. They want to check out your house.'

Ikem said that he knew of at least fifty Nigerians who had been deported despite having Chinese children. Some couples are forced to go to Nigeria for the requisite five years before returning to China. Others stay in Nigeria permanently. For some Chinese wives, life in Nigeria, with its humidity, mosquitoes and unfamiliar okra soup and cassava diet, is more than they can handle. Some return to China with their children, leaving their husbands behind until the five years are up. Meanwhile, unmarried Americans can get ten-year visas due to an agreement between the US and China.

'I'm not having that against them,' Ikem said of the Chinese government. 'This is their home. This is their land. And they wouldn't want any aliens to come and destroy their home.'

The Chinese government controls domestic movement among its own citizens too. As China modernises, millions of rural peasants are moving to the cities to find work. In order to regulate the flow of people entering the cities, the government introduced what is in essence a passport system, known as *hukou*. Rural Chinese cannot migrate to the cities without a hukou, and if they want anything such as a marriage licence, health insurance or a passport, they must return to their home village and apply from there. That includes urban-raised children who, once they reach high school age, must return to the village because that's where their hukou is located. It's an awful wrench for these teenagers, who have to leave behind friends and parents and join their grandparents in the sticks. Delinquency is a common consequence.

The restriction on the flow of migrants to the cities prevented the mushrooming of shanty towns and wealth inequality that have dogged cities in countries like India, Nigeria and Brazil, resulting in a relatively low crime rate in Chinese urban areas. This was the old communist ideal of putting society before the individual, head before heart, practicality over emotion. If the government can split Chinese families it stands to reason that it would do the same to African ones.

'I don't have a home, a place I love,' Ikem continued. 'You know, if you don't have a place you call your own and you're passionate about, life won't have much meaning to you. Even the animals are better than you, I'm telling you. Because the only thing that makes this life liveable, in my judgment, is passion. Of having something that you love so dear that you're ready to give everything to defend. You can say "family". Yes, but having a family is not what makes you human. It is your love for your nation. Let me make it clear: the Chinese people . . . you can be a friend to them . . . you can be a lover . . . you can be good to them . . . but if you don't love China – even if you're their husband, wife or business partner . . .'

My wristwatch battery had died. I handed it over to Ikem. As he changed the battery, he told me he had close Chinese friends. He would rather get drunk with a Chinese person than with a Nigerian, for the most dramatic of reasons: 'Nigerians – the Fulani and Yoruba peoples – want me dead,' he said, referring to the different ethnic groups. 'No Chinese wants me dead.

'Anywhere you are, the respect you command comes from where you come from . . . your home. Here in China, if I go to immigration for my visa processing, they see my passport and they know that I'm from this country. They limit options if you're Nigerian. You're in the black book . . . because you're from Damnation.'

Ikem's friend, a man named Chinedu, sat down next to me and nodded in agreement. Both he and Ikem said they kept AK-47s at home in Nigeria, which they disparagingly referred to as a 'zoo'. When Chinedu learned that my father had been a peaceful human rights activist, he told me that nothing had ever been solved through peace. Violence, he believed, was the only way to deal with zoo animals: 'The zoo is killing us so we must defend ourselves. Only in China we can sit here in peace like this. In Nigeria you are looking here and here,' he made mock furtive glances. Chinedu would fire his AK-47 in the air when he suspected intruders on his property in Nigeria.

'You must possess your possessions,' he said. 'An elephant may behave well but a lion will not.' This was not a Nigeria I'm familiar with, the gun ownership. Most people don't own those sorts of weapons. Ikem and Chinedu's lives in Nigeria seemed fraught with unspoken struggles or trauma. Perhaps for them China was a place of refuge, not just a destination for economic migration.

I told Ikem that I myself had problems getting a Chinese tourist visa – I was initially given just a sixteen-day visa instead of the standard thirty days for British passport holders, and I was livid about it.

'You don't get angry,' Ikem advised. 'You just have to do something to your identity. To clean it and become OK. If you are OK, respect is reciprocal. You don't ask for respect, you command it. At immigration I tell them I'm not a Nigerian. I tell them that I am from Biafra. They will know that Biafra existed before Nigeria.'

Ikem's wife was a quiet Guangzhou woman with strong, almost northern Chinese features. I saw her just once, briefly. Their eight-year-old daughter and six-year-old son were eating noodles in the shop. Both kids had Ikem's full lips and their mother's epicanthic eye folds. Under China's then one-child policy Ikem had to pay the government US$20,000 in order to register their son and have him recognised by the government.

Ikem's children were comparing heights, standing back-to-back and bantering in Chinese while their father watched and chuckled. Sometimes Ikem addressed them in Chinese, other times in English, though their grasp of the latter was very shaky. They spoke no Igbo. For all his Biafra talk, Ikem hadn't imposed much of his culture on his children. They had been born in China, schooled in China, their cradles rocked by their Chinese grandma.

Both kids recoiled from my iPhone lens yet basked in the focus of my big DSLR camera, as if the latter were somehow less intrusive. The girl grabbed the camera from me and began using it. She had a particularly good eye, examining a line of mannequins and working out a composition before taking a shot. The results were surprisingly good. Then her brother had a go and snapped a burly Nigerian man, who took exception to being photographed.

'Use that ting again and I will break it, o,' the man scowled. His eyes bulged like a raging bullfrog. He snatched my camera out of the boy's hands and scanned the jpegs before handing it back to me. I comforted the boy who by now had burst into tears.

I watched as Ikem's children played badminton with their Chinese friends in a central courtyard in the building. When a child is registered with the authorities, their ethnicity has to be stated. There is no box for 'mixed-race'.

'Do your daughter's friends see her as Chinese?' I asked Ikem.

'They think she's special, she's different. She's been loved, but they don't know that she's attached to a corrupt land. When they get to your age, when they know those attachments they will treat her differently. The society will want to find out where she comes from before they can accept her. "If she's Nigerian, is she going to defraud me? Can I leave her in my house?"'

According to the journalist Jenni Marsh, Chinese prejudice against Africans is normally based on traditional aesthetic values, an ignorance of African culture and society, and the language barrier. The notion of a Chinese person with sub-Saharan ancestry is hard for many to swallow.

A famous case was the uproar when a half-Black girl entered the Chinese version of *Pop Idol*, the television singing contest. Lou Jing, daughter of a Chinese woman and an African-American man, was raised single-handedly by her mother in Shanghai. Standing on the stage in a yellow dress, her face partially covered by a mask, she rapped in Chinese to a clapping audience. She then took off the mask, revealing a beautiful, relatively dark-skinned visage, with oriental eyes and the pronounced cheekbones of her African ancestors. The Chinese blogosphere went crazy. 'Wrong parents, wrong skin colour, wrong to be in a television show!' one commentator screamed. 'Little black devil'; 'Unwanted bastard' of a 'shameless whore'.

Her mother had an extramarital affair with an African American and her husband later divorced her. Women who have illicit affairs with white men are not condemned quite so vociferously. Lou Jing withstood the abuse (she also had many supporters) and made it to the top five before being eliminated. Afterwards, Shanghai television station Dragon TV offered her an internship and she went on to co-host a local Shanghai programme called News Surfing Intelligence.

The Chinese reaction to Africans like Lou Jing was under-pinned partly by a contempt of dark skin – they even discriminate against their darker-hued compatriots – and partly from a nativism that disdains everything non-Chinese, regardless of race. There's a current of anti-Islam that gets conflated with Africans, possibly because the first Africans to migrate to China were Muslims from Mali. Then there's a specific anti-African prejudice, rooted in the seductive but incorrect theory that Africa's economic underperformance is the result of an inherent inferiority of its people. Many have been fed the line that China is the benefactor and Africa the grateful recipient in Sino-African relations, though in reality China benefits more. The average Chinese person knows little about the positive contributions of African migrants to trade relations between the two regions. Compounding it all is a lack of exposure to Africans and the continent itself, not to mention the government's official assertion that racism does not exist in China.

There were open-minded people too, of course. The anthropologist Shanshan Lan cites online commentators such as this one: 'Please do not discriminate against blacks. Blacks have similar family values as us. Many of them are smart people . . . Black Africa has so much oil and national gas. Because of this we need to maintain good relations.'

Shanshan Lan says that overseas Chinese tend to be more ambivalent in their views. Some are against anti-African racism because of their personal experiences of discrimination at the hands of white people. Others tap into Western colonial discourses about Africans to fuel their anti-Black prejudice.

China's policy towards foreigners has had the sort of hard-line, ethnic-based rigidity that right-wing Westerners can only dream of. The Han ethnic group, which originated in Northern China and gave birth to Chinese civilisation, comprises 92 per cent of the Chinese population. Yet ironically, for all its ethnicity-based citizenship criteria, Tibetans, Uighurs, the Hlai and other non-Han ethnicities have been corralled under its One China umbrella, a notion best illustrated in a painting of the eighteenth-century Emperor Shizong of Qing. Keen to demonstrate his open and 'inclusive' attitude towards religions, the emperor commissioned a series of paintings portraying him dressed in costumes from various cultures within his empire. He is seen imitating a Buddhist monk, a Taoist priest, a Tibetan lama and even a European (complete with curly wig). Whether he would have gone so far as to wear African robes is debatable. Chinese identity is based on an outward expansion of the Chinese territory and assimilation of peripheral tribes into the core Chinese ethnicity and culture. Outsiders wanting to become Chinese citizens don't get a look-in – not even the more highly regarded Europeans.

However, Ikem the jeweller was fixated on the idea that he could elevate his status in China by shedding his Nigerian identity and becoming a citizen of a new ethnic-Igbo nation.

'Do you know that if you come from an independent Biafra, the Chinese who denied you your visa, do you know they will not deny you that based on your identity anymore? Your identity will not say that you are a Nigerian anymore. But if you have a reference to a corrupt entity like Nigeria the stigma is following you everywhere. The problems will follow you and last forever. The stigma will follow your children.'

Arguing with Ikem was futile. He was essentially fleeing his own shadow: most Africans in China are Nigerians, and most of those Nigerians are Igbo or 'Biafrans'. Within Nigeria, the Igbo reputation for entrepreneurial success contained the usual mixture of good and bad players. I sympathised with Ikem's desire to focus on the positive side of the story, but he was suffering from the cognitive dissonance of nationalistic mythology – British 'fair play', American 'freedom for all'. But I felt for him. To be judged by your nation – especially when that nation is Nigeria – can have life-limiting consequences. Personally, I just wanted to be judged for being me.

—

Days later I witnessed this anti-Igbo sentiment first-hand. I was in the Xiaobei neighbourhood of Guangzhou again, a couple of miles away from the Sanyuanli district. I was here to get some African grub. A Liberian man had recommended I come to Baohan Straight Street near the Donfranc Hotel, an area where, as the Liberian put it, they 'try' to make African food. Passing the Moustache African Food restaurant, I saw an African man barking at a Chinese waitress for 'more onion, more tomato'. He didn't sound satisfied.

I settled on a Uighur restaurant opposite a shop called Cause of Glad Shoes. It served Arabic, Pakistani, Indian and African food and drew a corresponding clientele. Plump stomachs, thighs spread wide, kufi hats and a throaty babel of Swahili, Mandingo, pidgin English, Urdu and Arabic; pale marble floors, Arabic script tapestries hanging from marble walls; a prayer room by the toilets. I was pretty much the only person in there who wasn't male and Muslim and hollering abrupt requests at the waitresses ('Water!' 'Glass!' 'Chapati!' 'Bring bread!'). Was their gruffness a sexist thing or a non-native-English-speaker thing? Perhaps both.

The waitresses soaked up the demands stoically. They teamed their pious lace headscarves and long-sleeved sweaters with tight leather trousers and mid-heel leather boots, and they smiled in appreciation at my gentler, more polite requests. I struck up brief conversations with Liberians and

Congolese and Zambians, but nothing interesting was said. They were either too busy, too concise or too condescending, crafting simplistic responses to my questions. Men bellowed down their phones, arranging to pick up goods or discussing currency exchange rates. Three South Asian men watched a Bollywood film on the wall-mounted TV. Set in nineteenth-century Rajasthan, the colonial British soldiers were shot and stabbed by an Indian protagonist. Those actors were the only white people I saw that day (real-life Europeans were rare sightings in Xiaobei and Sanyuanli – they tended to be clustered around Guangzhou's more upmarket neighbour-hoods such as Panyu towards the south of the city).

The film and the restaurant represented a cultural axis, which, if I'm honest, brought on a certain anxiety. It was male-dominated, sexist, gruff. My Black, female self was reduced to an even smaller speck than usual. Some commen-tators celebrate this sort of axis, a world without the West's mediation or cultural hegemony. Was that such a good thing from my perspective? 'The West' may be shorthand for whiteness, but in reality it is home to Africans and other ethnic minorities who have helped shape and moderate Western society's values. And there was more emphasis on the rights of the individual, the recognition of individuals. For all its faults I had greater purchase in the West than among this restaurant crowd.

As I ordered my food from the waitress, a Pakistani guy at the next table interrupted and bellowed for her attention. I turned to face him: 'Excuse me, she's dealing with me first.' He piped down out of shock rather than obedience.

Soon an elegant-looking Nigerian lady glinting with jewel-lery came and shared my table. Fifty-something, refreshingly articulate, with a silvery Afro, her name was Tayo. We could barely hear ourselves speak over the din of the Urdu-language TV newscast coming from the screen above us.

Tayo rolled her eyes and smiled at me. She was in Guangzhou for a few days on business. She ran a small but multifaceted enterprise, selling ice cream, fruit juice machines and bespoke printed mugs.

'I take your picture, put it on the printer, print it out on paper, put it round the mug, put it in a mug press, and within fifteen to twenty minutes you see your face on the mug,' she said. (I remember those mugs, printed with a photo of the bride and groom, an image which, over the years, fades and crumbles in tandem with the passions of the marriage.) For years Tayo had been coming to China to buy the sublimation equipment. Her profit margins were diminishing yearly because of the naira–dollar exchange rate.

'So do you like China?' I asked her.

'For business, yes. But not for anything else. I can't live here.'

'Why?'

'They are not friendly.'

'I can't tell,' I told her. 'I don't know what they're thinking or what they're saying.'

Tayo lowered her voice. 'They are racist. They are not friendly. I think the people who can really cope with them are the people living here . . . the Igbos.'

'Why?'

'Because they too are . . . I think they are like them.'

As a neutral observer, the Igbo–Yoruba ethnic rivalry never ceases to amaze me. It plays out wherever the two find themselves, in a whispering continuation of the Biafran civil war. Members of both groups issue in-depth proclamations about one another's psyche. Given half a chance they'll pontificate with professorial certainty on the state of one another's underwear.

'You know, if you're not careful . . . I'm sorry, but the typical Igbo man wants to cheat you. And the same thing with these Chinese here, if you're not careful. They have four brands of quality. Four qualities in any item. That's why whatever I'm buying, I don't tell them I'm taking it to Nigeria. I tell them I'm sending my goods to a shipping company. They don't know where it's going. So I always tell them, "Give me your stock that is going to the UK or US or New Zealand." So that way I'm getting the best quality.'

'That's good to know!'

'You need to know that before you start importation. Our Igbo friends . . . our Igbo cousins . . . they come here and they get the lowest of the quality. Even when the Chinese are not offering the lowest, they tell the Chinese, "Give me the lowest of the quality."'

'They actually want the lowest?'

'Yes, so that they maximise the price and then the profit. So most of the things they bring into Nigeria are cheap quality. They know that in six months the product will collapse. That's why I say they and the Chinese are like-minds. And that's why they are able to flow and stay here.'

'I was wondering why nearly everyone I meet is Igbo,' I remarked. 'Where are all the Yorubas? An Igbo guy told me a theory about that—'

'—he gave you a cock-a-hoop story?' Tayo shifted agitatedly in her seat, ready for the challenge. 'So what did he say? Let me hear, now.' She threw her red shawl over her shoulder, her square jaw clenched with determination.

I told her how a man at Ikem's jewellery shop had claimed that Yoruba men let their women do all the work.

'Uh-uh, that is exactly what I expected him to say,' Tayo said, looking visibly ruffled. 'We have conscience, let me put it like that. We have conscience, and we have integrity. I don't want anybody to buy anything from my shop, come back in six months and say it's bad.

'They will tell you all sorts of stories. Look, I have a client in Abuja. She told me she bought an ice-cream machine from an Igbo guy in Apapa in Lagos. And that the thing was not cooling. She called the guy back, the guy said, "Ah, no it's no problem. Just call the guy, let them fill it with gas." Something she bought newly. Who is going to pay for the gas filling? The lady said that after about three weeks she told him to "refund my money". The guy refused to refund the money. And that's another thing with those Igbos, they don't refund the money. No matter how much you try.' Tayo rapped the table with her knuckle on each word for emphasis: 'They. Don't. Refund. Your. Money.'

'But then how do they stay in business? I don't understand.'

'Somehow they do. They don't refund their money. If you buy something from them and it doesn't work after a while they will tell you it is the electricity that has spoiled it. They tell you all sorts of stories. This lady now had to buy another ice-cream machine from me. In fact, she bought a used machine from me.'

'Do ordinary customers in Nigeria know that Igbo imports are low quality?'

'Of course they know. But unfortunately the Igbo are more into the business. In fact, if you get to Alaba electronics market in Lagos, before you see a Yoruba man in business you will see more than a hundred Igbo.'

Igbos are now said to make up 40 per cent of the population in Lagos, Nigeria's biggest city, even though it is situated in Yoruba territory. I told Tayo how when Igbos come to Guangzhou they approach other Igbo to help them get established. Did Tayo believe those Igbo immigrants would do the same for Nigerians of other ethnicities? She closed her eyes and shook her head. I then told her that when I posed this question to the Igbo guys, they said they would help anyone.

'And the story we heard – but I cannot confirm that – is that they all pledge an oath between them that they have to keep to. So that way, they help themselves. Igbo guys, they bring apprentices from home. Those guys will never mess around with them or cheat them or steal their money. Let the same guy go to a Yoruba man – it will be a different story. Even as the house help, they will steal your things, kill you. There was a driver—' Tayo stopped herself ' . . . let me not go into that.' She kissed her teeth and smiled. 'So they only owe obeisance to themselves.

'Awolowo* believed so much in education. And that's why our own fathers believe that even when he doesn't have any money he will send his children to school. An Igbo man believes that business is it. You can ask an Igbo man "What is two plus two?" and he doesn't know it is four. But tell

---

* Chief Obafemi Jeremiah Oyeniyi Awolowo was a Yoruba nationalist and Nigerian statesman who played a key role in Nigeria's independence movement. He was the first Premier of the Western Region under Nigeria's parliamentary system, from 1952 to 1959, and the official Leader of the Opposition in the federal parliament from 1959 to 1963.

him two dollars plus two dollars, he'll tell you four dollars. It's that bad.

'They believe it's all about business,' Tayo continued. 'That is why at age three, four or five, they put their children with somebody who is into business. By the time that boy is twenty they will ask the man to settle him. The guy is not paying him, he's just an apprentice. But they will have an agreement, maybe after spending ten years with you, you'll have to settle him. You set him up with a business, the same business he has learned over time with you.

'They prefer to send the girls to school than the men. The men will go into business at a very early age. And they don't get married early. So by the time they are getting married they may have a girlfriend and decide to send her to university. So at the end of the day it is that lady who will now be MD of his company. She is well read and will be able to take care of it. He will still be travelling and be doing everything. At the end of the day, the Igbo ladies get the best of it. I will tell you, the husband dotes on them. Apart from the huge money he pays for the dowry. Most times the families cannot refund the dowry, so that's why you see that there's very low divorce rates amongst the Igbo.'

I wasn't sure which parts to believe. Listening to various ethnic groups characterising each other with broad brush-strokes amused me endlessly. It didn't seem an Igbo thing, really. These business people were simply members of that international tribe of dodgy wheeler-dealers.

'This is the problem with Nigeria,' Tayo continued. 'We are still talking about this electricity. The cost of manufacturing in Nigeria. You can have a made-in-Nigeria product.

And yet the cost is so high. So you prefer to go out and bring it in. That's the basic problem we have. I remember at the University of Ife, there was a time when they manufactured machines that can do pounded yam. But even the one that I bought many years back is five times more expensive than the one here in China. It would not be making any sense to manufacture in Nigeria. When you start thinking about it, sometimes you get depressed, because you see the likes of people like me working so hard and yet we don't get anything.' Tayo paused and looked at me: 'So how much are you paying me for this interview and all this knowledge?'

I stared in disbelief.

Tayo burst out laughing. 'I scare you, ehn?'

Igbo traders are the source of much of the chagrin felt by consumers like Tayo over in Nigeria. Complaints over their shoddy goods were compounded by existing mistrust about them ever since Nigeria's civil war ended in 1970. I didn't share those feelings, especially as I live in London and don't have to contend with sub-standard imports. Being in Guangzhou for a couple of weeks gave me a more sympathetic perspective on Igbo traders, whose travails I was able to witness. They complained that it wasn't them but the Chinese who exploit customers in Sanyuanli.

Later that day, I stopped by Ikem's jewellery shop for the first time in a week. It was a social hub for Africans, and a good place for me to meet new people. I got chatting to Valentine, an Igbo man in his forties who had skinny legs and wore a woollen cap.

'They are just here to make noise,' he remarked contemptuously about other Nigerians in the neighbourhood.

'What do you mean "noise"?' I asked.

'Eighty per cent of people here are not focused. They just want to say they are going to China.'

Valentine sat on a table. The idle swinging of his bandy legs was a marked contrast to his professed industriousness. For someone with a business he seemed to have time on his hands that afternoon. For twelve years he had been coming to Guangzhou, and for the last three he based himself here, running a shipping logistics business for people exporting goods from Guangzhou. At his warehouse he had a vacuum pressing machine that could compress 2,000 pairs of jeans into a space the size of a 200-litre trunk.

This export business was fraught with insecurity for cargo handlers like Valentine. The standards of goods are much lower and piracy is a major risk. African consumers have had to get used to the risk of knock-offs and shoddy standards. Roughly 10 per cent of all goods to Africa are said to be exact 'copies'.

The Hong Kong-based anthropologist Gordon Mathews makes a distinction between copies and 'knock-offs'. 'Copies' are products made in Chinese factories that are exact replicas of branded goods, such as iPhones and Gucci bags, etc. By contrast knock-offs are replicas except they are given tiny but crucial variations in their name in order to obtain a degree of legal protection, e.g. 'Nokla', instead of Nokia, or 'Apply' rather than Apple. (I once read a funny news story about a woman from Wuxi who ordered an Apple iPhone 6 but received a 'Pear' phone instead from scammers.) Or the products have Chinese brand names or no name at all. And they're cheap.

Every now and then the Chinese government launches anti-piracy searches but they only check a quarter or a third of merchandise, and exporters often know when the inspections are taking place. Fines are around US$3,000–4,000, much of it going straight into the pockets of Chinese custom officers.

African cargo agents have a lot to worry about. There could be anything in those containers – porn, cocaine, guns. The customer who asks for a letter of invitation for a Chinese visa: is he or she a drugs mule? If the cargo agent collects a mule at the airport and she's later caught by the police, the agent is implicated and punished.

Valentine and I discussed the issue of fake goods in Guangzhou in general. He complained that Africans here are given some of the worst-quality products – even food.

'Sixty per cent of the things they are eating is not from the real company. It's a copy. They think nothing can kill an African man, you know? If you want to drink whiskey or beer in a bar in Sanyuanli, it is not the same whiskey or beer you will get in these other places. You know, in some popular African clubs what you see there is fake drink. People will buy it at the same price as the original one. When you drink it you come out and find out you are not feeling normal. Some of them are wicked. Most of the things they sell in the shops near Canaan Market are not real.'

I could attest to that. The second-hand phone I bought was real but the charger that accompanied it was a dud from the get-go.

'So when you go to a club are you careful about what you drink?' I asked.

'Yeah.'

'So I should never buy food in Sanyuanli?'

He shook his head. 'Go to a big shop. But don't buy from

local shops. Sometimes you can watch very carefully if the Chinese are not going there to buy. Before I used to smoke. I've stopped now. The cigarette they used to give was not real cigarette. The ministry in charge of those things may come and check. They will hide those fake ones or bribe the officials. When the Chinese person sees you now, the first thing they will think is to cheat you.'

—

Fake goods were the scourge of Nigeria, a wound to the soul of any prideful Nigerian. Every short-lived phone charger or chemically dubious mosquito coil, the Chinglish Google-translate gibberish on its packaging instructions, was a rebuke to our failed manufacturing sector and a slap in the face by Chinese manufacturers and their Nigerian trader middlemen. But although rich countries regard the fake goods trade as undermining and in need of policing, there are academics who think counterfeits are actually a benefit to the developing world.

Gordon Mathews thinks there are benefits to the 'fake' economy, i.e. moving fake goods across borders and continents illegally. He calls this activity 'globalisation from below', saying it is how most of the planet actually experiences globalisation. Fake goods, Mathews says, allow people in poorer countries to participate in the global economy. Rather than being in opposition to the formal economy, they are actually the natural outcome of World Bank and IMF-imposed neoliberal economic policies that serve big multinationals and widen wealth inequality. Fake goods stimulate a parallel economy that fills a gap in demand that would not otherwise be met. Most Africans can't afford smartphones at official retail prices, so 'globalisation from below' gives them access to otherwise unobtainable smartphones and other devices. They want 'a taste' of the good stuff (as a South African township dweller once told me). And, Mathews claims, the big manufacturers are surprisingly OK with it. He cites a Nokia employee who informed him that Nokia secretly turned a blind eye to knock-offs because the consumers might one day adopt the real thing if and when affluent enough. And denying such customers Nokia handsets of any sort might see an increase in thefts of the real product.

Low-income transnationalism like this also provides jobs and income in the developing world. The export of fake goods creates service industries and jobs in the informal economy, from street vendors to shipping companies and phone repairers. And through fake phones and computers, people acquire information from the internet, improving their linguistic and professional skills in a way that would have been harder under their poorly funded education systems. In many ways, fake products unite humanity. It's hard for me to imagine a world without social media or popular phone apps to stay in touch with friends and family in Nigeria. Globalisation from below, Mathews believes, will outlast the kind from above as the developed world moves from one financial crisis to the next. It is the future.

I wanted in on this fake goods party. When I needed a new lens for my camera, people in Guangzhou advised me to go to Dashatou, the city's biggest electronics market where goods were sold at a fraction of the UK price. Apple

MacBook copies were especially popular with foreign students.

The first stall I encountered by the entrance was manned by a woman idly picking her nose as she sat behind a forest of dildos. Further inside was where the magic began. I was in tech heaven. Electronic goods gleamed and winked at me beneath artificial lights. Many of them were genuine brands of proper quality (I bought a perfect Canon 18-200mm camera lens for half its UK retail price). Other items were good quality copies. Then there were the poor quality copies and knock-offs. Distinguishing between those different categories required powers I didn't have, and the vendors knew it. In this emporium of treachery, merchants polish and package their turds with a smile. It also put my own morality and strength to the test: I entered that place wanting nothing but a camera lens yet within seconds I was lusting after gadgets I didn't need – and I'm ashamed to say I was prepared to buy fakes.

The gods rightly punished me for it.

I bought the (then latest) iPhone 8 – Apple of my eye – from a woman in whose eyes I thought I saw a benevolent soul. We had chatted about our families while I cuddled her toddler; we discussed food and the beauty of Yangshuo – a place I wanted to visit – and how its limestone karsts feature on Chinese banknotes. There was a bond between us, I thought. Having sought advice from a passing Indian customer who assured me the phone was legit, I handed over US$85. Although I had tested the phone's various features, I stupidly forgot to test the camera. Later that evening, back at my hotel room, I took a test photo and almost cried at the blur of gigantic pixels on the screen. I had been cheated.

Experiences like these have a way of correcting your moral compass very quickly.

I'm amazed that the Chinese, with all their manufacturing capabilities, are still willing to buy Western brands at all. They could easily produce their own. The British opium pushers of the nineteenth century would never have guessed that China would desire something non-narcotic from Westerners and that this desire lay not in the tangibility of a manufactured item but in the arbitrary rules of style and taste, from the Louis Vuitton houndstooth pattern, the iconic Gucci double 'G' logo, the Burberry tartan or an Oxford University degree. Western power hangs by a soft thread of brand cachet. One wonders if and when the Chinese will snip that thread.

Meanwhile, in Africa, they want our natural resources.

III

PEOPLE MOUNTAIN
PEOPLE SEA

At Guangzhou Railway Station dozens of people were lining up to enter. The queue spilled out beyond the station exit and onto the streets. The size and density of the crowd resembled a stadium event, except many were sitting down. Hunched on small portable stools, they had flasks of hot water which they poured into pots of instant noodles. Their clothes and haircuts looked shabby. Having not read the news in a few days I was oblivious to what was going on. It was the Chinese New Year, a holiday that had crept up on me unawares as I hadn't done my research. It turned out that these people were factory workers, the labourers responsible for making so much of the world's consumer goods and clothes. They were returning to their rural homes to spend Chinese New Year with their families, as part of the meagre eleven days' annual leave they were entitled to.

It's one of the greatest human migrations in the world, with hundreds of millions of people pouring out of the big industrial cities and heading back to their villages each year. A whole year of stored-up passions – one chance to show love, share laughs, settle feuds. Guangzhou Railway Station was the main gateway out of the city.

However, heavy snow in the central and eastern provinces had created delays on the trains, producing an almighty logjam of passengers. At one point, fifty thousand people were stranded at the station, some of them waiting days for a seat on a train out of Guangdong Province. The inconvenience of it all might have triggered unrest elsewhere in the world but this crowd accepted their fate with the equanimity of people whose modest expectations of life matched the reality. I was particularly taken by an older man with a tousle of silver hair, trimmed beard and scruffy trousers, who sat on some folded mats. Spine straight, arms clasped around crossed legs, eyes closed, he was a picture of poise and serenity. I took a photo of him.

It took days for the crowds to dissipate, but once they finally did they left behind a city that was startlingly empty, a post-apocalyptic wasteland. I wandered the streets like an urban hunter-gatherer, foraging for takeaway food. Most shop windows were covered up behind metal shutters. That, combined with the indecipherable Chinese shop names, lent the neighbourhood a strange anonymity and uniformity.

A handful of hardy shop owners in Sanyuanli stayed open to profit from their few remaining African customers. Many Africans had gone back to the continent for the holidays, but the visa overstayers were trapped here, of course. I encountered a group of them in the empty Guangyuanxi Road, standing among wind-blown leaflets. They were spouting ridiculous conspiracy theories in loud Nigerian voices while a cute little Afro-Chinese boy swung playfully around their legs.

As usual, I needed a haircut. Thankfully and predictably,

one of the men was a barber, ready to snip. He was a Nigerian who had become a naturalised Liberian ('Any passport is better than Nigerian passport'). The man whipped out his kit, pulled out a chair for me to sit in there on the pavement, wrapped a sheet around my shoulders and handed me a small mirror to hold. The breeze blew stray hairs over my face.

'Piàoliang!' an elderly Chinese passer-by shouted, giving me a thumbs-up. 'Pretty!'

For the third time in two days I ate at the Uighur restaurant, one of the few decent eateries still open in the area. But I was bored of it. Bored of Uighur rice and mutton, bored of talking to men who, although kind, were often laconic. All those with valid visas had flown home or were resting indoors. I felt confined in their world, in this portion of the city. There was little reason for me to hang around Guangzhou over the festive period yet I was nervous about leaving. I felt comfortable here. Its African community made it feel like a home away from home. And the Chinese people here were accustomed to our presence. That didn't mean they were always friendly, but at least they didn't gawp at me as if I were alien. I wondered what it would be like to travel alone as a Black person in the rest of China where the Africans were rare or non-existent. The prospect was daunting but I was up for the challenge. I was dying to see other parts of this country, whose 5,000-year civilisation was as deep as its mountains were high.

—

It didn't take long for me to get a taste of life as an African outside of Guangzhou's cosmopolitan bubble. At the airport check-in line, four members of a family who were waving off a relative stood and watched my face as if I were a television. Only the popcorn was missing. My blood pressure was up already, but it was the price I was willing to pay to get an eyeful of China's stunning provincial scenery.

I arrived in Zhangjiajie, in Hunan Province. Through the taxi windows I saw its blue-grey mountain peaks shrouded in a cold mist.

Seeing the sights in China is not for the faint-hearted. An expanding middle class has turned tourism into an insanely crowded business, especially during holiday time, in a phenomenon known as *ren shan ren hai*, meaning 'people mountain people sea'. Tourist sites were log-jammed with domestic visitors who were as fascinated by their own country as anyone else. I soon learned that sightseeing was a mission not a holiday, its rigours almost as demanding as any factory job. It required very early starts, for one. Setting my alarm before 6 a.m. the next morning seemed a clever idea, but when I was jolted awake half an hour prematurely by Chinese guests clod-hopping down the hotel stairwell and chatting, I realised what I was up against: whatever game or strategy you think you've invented, the people of this nation came up with it a thousand years before. I scissor-kicked the duvet off me and hurried into the shower.

Tianmen Mountain was the first place I wanted to visit. Getting there involved travelling on the world's longest cable car ride, but first I had to join the world's longest queue. A line of people stretched thirty metres ahead and folded along several hairpin bends. A mawkish muzak tune emanated from overhead speakers – the same sixteen bars on a torturous loop. People projected their voices loudly and directionlessly despite standing cheek-by-jowl (a hangover, some say, from rural days when farmers shouted across the rice paddies to one another).

The smell of cigarettes and the sound of spitting forced me to close my eyes and 'think of England', except keeping them closed for too long resulted in someone sidling ahead of me. Maintaining one's position in the queue required Formula 1-style tactics: overtake on the inside, round the hairpin bend, then switch sides for the next round of inside overtaking. There was no room for decorum. Without guile and trickery you were left behind. When four gangster-looking types with gelled quiffs and upturned jacket lapels jumped fifty places ahead, nobody seemed outraged by the infraction. Nor were they troubled by the lack of personal space. Daylight between bodies was considered a waste of real estate. People were numb to my angry jostles each time they pressed up behind me. Yet over time I myself started thrusting against the person ahead because if I didn't inhale their hair or hump their arse someone else would squeeze in and do it for me.

By now we had been standing for three hours – enough time for me to convert to five different religions and beg each deity for strength. I needed even more psychological strength when the lady in front of me turned around to watch a TV screen suspended from the ceiling. The elegance of her bobbed hair, yellow coat and lipstick won my admiration – until she yawned in my face at point blank range without covering her mouth. I might have been felled by that spicy hurricane were it not for the man pressed so tightly behind me that he was supporting my entire bodyweight.

Ninety minutes later I finally collapsed into a seat in a cable car and began a seven-mile ascent towards clouds speared by sparkling sunrays. It felt like a stairway to heaven. Perhaps I really had died of exhaustion and was about to meet God.

The mountain loomed close and the cable ascended steeply over sheer cliffs towards one of the mountain peaks. We soared above the 99 Bends, a serpentine road that wound up the mountain in hairpin turns, flanked by beautifully crenellated walls. I reached the top of the mountain at an altitude of 1,500 metres. The forty peaks of the Tianmen range loomed around us, faded behind clouds of mist. This was the China I had longed to see, the bucolic calm of ancient photos. Nestled between two peaks was Tianmen ('Heaven's Door'), an oblong hole in the cliff face, carved by water over millions of years. On a cloudless day the sun's rays spread outwardly from this natural arch, creating a visual so luminous it could challenge the most ardent non-spiritualist. I was transfixed. But I soon learned that the yin of such beauty was accompanied by the yang of domestic tourism – a man came and stood next to me, leaned over the railing and spat into the valley. We both watched his gob fall one thousand feet.

I joined the hoards and shuffled along the cliff-hanging glass walkway, one of the highest in the world. It was suspended high up in the air and had a glass floor that gave vertigo-inducing views of the valley floor. There's a lot of this sort of thing in China. Thrill-seeking installations; high bridges, transparent flooring.

At the end of the walkway an official camerawoman screamed at each of us to smile and wave at her lens, whether we wanted to or not. I was cold and a little overwhelmed by the drill-march vibe of it all, but I raised my hand nonetheless and manufactured a smile. Retrieving the photos was – without exaggeration – the closest I have come to being in a rugby scrum. Approximately a dozen tourists were crowded around two outdoor PC monitors. Each had to identify their photo thumbnail, request a printout of it and then retrieve the printout. They pushed and shoved and squeezed against one another to find their image. It was so crowded I couldn't catch even a glimpse of the monitor.

Luckily, a random man signalled to me that my thumbnail was showing on the screen. Being the only dark face made me easy to spot (Blackness had its advantages, finally). The computer lady held my photo printout towards me, but as I moved to collect it somebody's arm knocked my temple. My torso was yanked to the left, my head to the right. A mass of jostling limbs blocked my vision almost entirely. The mob jerked and swayed in every direction, pushing, fighting, grunting and squealing. It took me a while but I eventually fought my way into daylight, grabbed the photograph and staggered away in a dishevelled fluster, straightening out my coat and earrings. I inspected the photo of me waving happily at the camera. An image can tell a thousand lies.

Continuing along the snowy mountain path, I saw women negotiate the icy path in high-heel boots, which they teamed with handbags, bangles and fitted jackets. Their wardrobe was thoroughly unsuitable but this was not so much a sightseeing trip as an affirmation of their lifestyle upgrade. Barely did they take in the scenery or pause for quiet contemplation: extend selfie stick, smile and flick the V-sign, then move on.

At what point, I wondered, will domestic tourism reach full capacity in this country? Each year the urban middle class grows, but the supply of attractions isn't increasing with the rising demand (a news website reported that half a million people visited Hangzhou's West Lake in one day). At what point will people think, *It's too crowded, let's do something else*. Perhaps never – especially if their idea of a fun day out is defined by posing in front of an object. They'll wait all day to achieve that. Their excitement was infectious nonetheless. Under Mao's communism, people had laboured with little reward, but now hard work finally had a tangible payoff – these people had urban homes, disposable incomes and could travel recreationally. I liked that.

But my positivity evaporated when, further along the mountain, I stood on a wooden hanging bridge that swayed considerably above the valley floor, only for a grown man to test its strength by stamping repeatedly on the planks, making my knees and camera lens wobble. I had to abandon all attempts to photograph the valley, beautiful as it was.

—

Early the next morning, I travelled ten kilometres north from Zhangjiajie city and found myself alone in a sub-tropical wonderland of quartzite sandstone peaks, eroded by wind and water and rising like needles from the misty valley floor. There were thousands of them, hundreds of feet high, each one topped with trees and vegetation. This was Zhangjiajie National Forest Park, one of the most stunningly beautiful landscapes on earth. I was in the Wulingyuan Scenic Area, specifically, and on a misty day, the rock pillars are largely obscured, revealing only the top sections, which appear to float above the clouds like islands. They are said to be the inspiration behind the iconic floating islands seen in the Hollywood movie *Avatar*.

Nearby, a forest of redwood trees rustled with the calls of macaques. I meditated in the midst of this serenity, walking for miles along the floor of the Baizhuang valley, over bridges and streams where giant salamanders once slithered en masse but are now critically endangered. Along the way, people kindly offered to take photos of me on my camera. I was mobbed by crowds of smiling parents and children requesting a photo op with me. One family thrust their five-year-old boy into my arms. The kid was small and heavy, like a cannonball, and looked as pissed off as I was about our enforced intimacy. He burst into tears and wriggled out of my arms. Others pointed at my short, Afro hair and gave me the thumbs up, calling me 'Michelle Obama' and insisting on adopting a frozen handshake pose with me as if I were America's First Lady. I didn't mind the attention – it happened to most foreigners, regardless of their ethnicity.

A blonde friend of mine received the same treatment on her visit to China. 'I was probably trending on Weibo that day,' she joked. Let's hope the online comments were kind. Two hundred years ago these Chinese folk might have done what the Europeans did and kept me in a cage for public viewing. Perhaps the online jpeg was the modern incarnation of that cage? I wavered between paranoia and warmth. Paranoia set in when the occasional child whispered something about me to their parents and the parents returned conspiratorial smiles. And my goodwill was tested when certain men went out of their way to squeeze past me no matter where I stood, despite obvious alternative routes. Were they trying to *smell* me?

As I drew lingering looks, I wondered what emotion lay

behind those eyes. Admiration, intrigue or disgust? I couldn't be sure. A constant tittering lingered in my wake, which I angrily interpreted as childish. There's a chance they weren't being juvenile – foreign cultural traits can mistakenly seem puerile to the beholder (many Chinese find Westerners' weak filial piety and penchant for short-term gratification a sign of immaturity, for example). Still, I grew impatient with the whispers on my approach, especially those women who liked to cover their mouths with one hand (as if I could lip-read their dialect) while pointing at me with the other. Body language is universal, I wanted to scream at them.

Controlling my anger was difficult but imperative. I might have been the first Black person they had encountered in the flesh. Representing my haplogroup meant rising above whatever insults were falling on my deaf, monoglot ears, and playing the 'noble savage'. Even when a small crowd gathered round to watch me eat, I smiled back and munched on.

Nonetheless, it is galling to be Black, middle class and the object of derision. You hate these onlookers' constructed hierarchies and your lowly place within them. You're tempted to counteract it with a constructed hierarchy of your own: *I'm more educated and worldly than you*, you growl inwardly. But then you chide yourself in the face of such ugly snobbery – we are all cut from the same cloth. And yet your egalitarianism is not reciprocated; these people are looking down on you all the same.

Ultimately, my inner optimist took the endless selfie requests and handshakes as a triumph of our shared humanity.

Photography in the smartphone age came with other complications. I carried a DSLR camera everywhere, with the aim of taking candid shots of people. Except the subjects of my photos were photographers themselves now that everyone has a phone camera these days. On seeing me they would whip out their phones to capture me snapping them, the pair of us creating a sort of infinity mirror reflection. Frustrating as it was, I couldn't complain. By virtue of possessing a 'proper' camera I assumed the role of photographer and they my subjects, but there were no rules about these things. One ultimately had to give in and smile.

I spent the next two days taking in the stunning scenery. Men roared periodically into the canyon to test the echo effect, and adults and children chucked food towards dustbins with unambitious aim, or fed the macaques in defiance of signs prohibiting it. The stereotype I held of China as a nation of conscientiousness and discipline died a little that day. But I had to get used to it. This was China. The government was pulling people out of rural poverty and into middle-class brackets, modernising at a lightning pace. It was as if rural peasants from the 1970s had been time-warped into the twenty-first century.

My friend, the British-born, Hong Kong-raised former shoe designer Beatrix Ong, told me she once met a lady who, sometime around 2005, was living in the countryside and had to cycle five miles to the next village to make a landline telephone call, yet within a few years that same woman was living in Beijing and using a smartphone.

The Chinese new-money tourist class have gained global infamy with their antics at home and abroad. Websites reported airline passengers tossing coins into plane engines prior to take-off as a good luck charm to protect against danger. There were the tourists who ravaged cherry trees in Nanjing in order to get selfies – a man kicked a tree in order to create a blossom shower, while a woman in killer heels climbed the lower branches and posed with a gleeful grin, her skirt riding up her thigh. I saw older passengers emptying tea from their flasks into garbage bins in airports.

In 2015, Chinese visitors to Mount Rigi in the Alps upset other passengers with their noise and spitting to the extent that the railway company created a separate carriage for them. 'Their strong presence,' said the railway chief, 'is a challenge.'

The Japanese government went so far as to create a special pamphlet, advising Chinese tourists on how to behave while visiting their country. In characteristic Japanese fashion, the phrasing was delicate and diplomatic; meanwhile the Chinese government issues etiquette guidance of its own, albeit with a blunter approach.

The nation's new sightseers have joined a long and rich tradition of emergent tourist classes committing faux pas around the world, beginning with English toffs defacing ancient Egyptian tombs with graffiti, and their lager-lout 1980s successors leaving puddles of vomit on the pavements of coastal Spain ('painting the town orange', if you will).

I wondered whether this irritation with Chinese domestic holidaymakers is underpinned partly by a disdain for tourism's arrivistes, the kind of snobbery that conflates with our desire for exclusivity and the conceit that travelling is an act of sophistication. The mass tourist destroys that illusion.

Perhaps people aren't accustomed to the sounds of a new language and ethnicity dominating the sightseeing arena. White travellers can colonise a site without drawing as much disapproval. They are the wallpaper of our consciousness, ubiquitous and unchallenged in a way that the Chinese are not.

If I'm honest with myself, their 'bad' habits are a bit subjective and open to bias. To my ears they spoke too loudly – but languages have a way of sounding louder when they're foreign and unintelligible. Nigerians and Brits could be just as noisy in their speech.

Annoying as some Chinese tourists' habits sometimes were, I loved their wonderment and enthusiasm for this exciting new world. I envied it. China's trajectory of shaky but steady economic growth is the envy of the West where the younger generation is poorer than their parents, productivity has stagnated, the optimism gone. Although those same storm clouds are gathering over China's economy, and its demographic time bomb ticks loudly, there's still an expectation that the rural poor can look forward to an upgraded standard of living in later generations.

In the meantime, their cultivated compatriots watch between fingers and cringe at their tarnished reputation in the same way the British once cringed at their rowdy kin on holiday in the first two decades of mass tourism in Mediterranean Europe.

—

I was heading to Yangshuo in Guangxi Province, which is unquestionably one of the most gobsmackingly beautiful places on earth. The train shot through the Guangdong Province countryside at 343km/h on elevated tracks. The speed and altitude altered the scale of the landscape and affected my depth perception, making the people working on the sheet-mirror rice paddies appear much smaller than expected.

The train pulled into Guilin in the province of Guangxi, and from there I took a taxi to Yangshuo County further down the Li River. We coursed down the highway, through a breathtaking landscape of limestone karsts, those geological formations that resemble giant, verdant cones. Dozens of these karsts were scattered around for miles, like an irregular and jagged egg tray.

For centuries artists and poets have painted and waxed lyrical about this mystical landscape. The Tang dynasty poet Han Yu described it as a place where 'the river winds like a green silk ribbon, while the hills are like jade hairpins'. Its forested peaks feature in so many Chinese tourist-board photos, often foregrounded with faux-Luddite cormorant fishermen wearing rice hats. Hackneyed imagery, yes, but it never gets old – those mountains are too magical and too big. Literally and figuratively, they rise above the modern-day tourist hoards and dwarf the pestilential helicopters that give wealthy tourists what must be stunning aerial views.

I arrived in Yangshuo and checked into a hotel managed by a young guy who was standing in temporarily for his sister. He insisted on giving me an old and tattered street map of the city, and requested that I return it, even though a stack of fresh, disposable maps were piled on the table for other guests – whites, of course – to use and keep. When I insisted he give me a new map he acquiesced very reluctantly. Experiencing racism in a place where you can't speak the language is so frustrating. I cursed him under my breath.

For the next two days I rented a bike and cycled through Yangshuo and its beautiful surrounds. Sometimes I rode on the wrong side of the road, just as I had seen other cyclists and motorised rickshaws do. There was no outraged honking from motorists. They seemed to accept that cycling against the flow of traffic was a practical decision that caused no harm.

I took a walk towards Moon Hill, a limestone cave that has eroded to the extent that it is now a hole within a flattened, triangular arch of rock; then I trundled along the Li River where brides-to-be posed for photographs before walking off while lifting up their wedding dresses to reveal black jeans and trainers underneath. Towards sunset I boarded a narrow bamboo raft that glided along the river, slicing through the karsts, backed by golden rays. The river fish have been depleted to the extent that ordering fish in restaurants will set you back US$40.

For dinner I selected restaurants almost at random. In one place where friendly, gangster-looking men posed with me for selfies, their stubbly faces close enough to mine that I could smell their cigarette breath. And I weighed up the pros and cons of either sticking to the safe chicken dishes of the night before or hazarding the 'Good Taste Beef Offal', 'Lijiang River Fish fry acid' or 'Acmaeas Burst Frog' on the menu. In the end I chickened out (pardon the pun) and ate my usual under the darting eyes of a girl of about seven who left her family's table to 'inspect' the cloth on an empty table near mine.

The next day I met my walking guide, a local woman named Lilly, who was friendly, chatty and spoke some English, a rarity in these parts. We drove to the village on the edge of Putao, a quiet, unassuming place of concrete houses set among rice fields. Lilly led me to the crest of a hill from where we enjoyed the stunning landscape: sinuous rivers and valleys, a patchwork of crop fields, and isolated peaks and groups of peaks, shrouded in mist like an ancient painting. Lilly was so used to this scenery she told me she never knew exactly what visitors like me were photographing until we explained it to her. 'All this,' I said, pointing to a seemingly endless vista of karsts that stretched for what seemed like a million miles into the distance. I had never seen anything like it.

From our elevated height we could see villages isolated from one another by the soaring rock formations. Lilly told me that during World War Two, people fled into these scattered pockets to hide from the Japanese, which is why one still finds small villages lying in remote areas. We climbed down from the chilly hilltop and entered the sleepy village of Putao where new buildings were under construction; a mix of agriculture and rubble. The temple was one of the few old-looking buildings left.

The residents were old, the young people having left for the cities. Women played majong and men sat by the river and gazed at it. Lilly and I stopped by at the house of a very elderly man who looked supremely comfortable in padded pyjamas, padded gloves and padded socks. He sat silently in a chair by the threshold of his abode and stared out into the silent village while he let me photograph his living quarters. On the wall was a very large poster containing a highly saturated, almost cartoon-like, illustration of eight Communist Party officials mounted on horses. The old man was clearly still a supporter of the regime and had lived through several tumultuous decades. Sadly, he had no energy to talk about what he had witnessed in his lifetime. It was in places like these that the Great Leap Forward of the late 1950s played out, when farmers were banned from cultivating for private use; when government officials took the little produce farmers managed to grow and handed it over to their superiors, pretending it was 'surplus' and leaving the villagers to starve to death. These days Putao's agriculture is more commercial, the local farmers partially swapping rice cultivation in favour of growing decorative plants or tangerines, which are popular 'good luck' gifts around New Year. The water buffalo that once tilled the fields have gone too, having been replaced by rice harvesting machines. Same yields but quicker to reap, Lilly told me.

—

The hotel manager invited me to a special New Year's Eve dinner the next evening. Not a friendly gesture, mind, but a meal for guests costing US$60 per head. Traditionally, families considered pork a luxury. They would save up to buy a pig and slaughter it for the elders at New Year's. That feast had now expanded to include every type of meat on the planet, cooked by a kind-eyed elderly lady. I sat in the middle of the dining table alongside other hotel guests who were all Chinese – an older guy, a long-haired woman and her heavily built boyfriend. Apart from the couple we were all strangers to one another.

The food was prepared on a hot plate on the table. It was an orgy of animal flesh, no vegetables, just a few tasty dumplings in between several meat courses, served in a haze of hot steam and sizzles. The chicken soup was delicious; the cow's stomach, not so much. The duck was flavoursome but it came after the pig's thigh, which was horrendous.

Dinner was served in quantities so massive it very nearly

became the Last Supper. My stomach was stretched to bursting; I feared for my survival. Still, I tried finishing everything in front of me to avoid causing offence (and to justify the money I had paid). The food dishes kept on arriving at the table. The fish literally had no taste and slid down my throat like dry muesli. The older guy sitting to my right chewed loudly between drags on a cigarette, its smoke neutralising the smell of his meaty belches. At least his gases found an escape. Mine didn't. I clutched my bloated stomach and stifled a groan. Nobody knew each other or spoke any English, so we all perused our phones in silence. Etiquette seemed to allow for it, which I liked.

I soon excused myself, waddled back to my room, capsized onto my bed, and made a New Year's resolution never to eat food again. All around me was the sound of firecrackers being set off outside. Traditionally they were made from bamboo sticks and used to scare away evil spirits. Now they are industrial strength and insanely loud. I had spent the earlier part of the day terrified by these random detonations, which had me hurrying down the street like a medieval peasant fleeing a solar eclipse. As midnight and the New Year approached, all of Yangshuo was setting off the damn things. The sound pounded the skies, saturated my hotel building, closed in on my room itself and bludgeoned my brain.

I inserted my earplugs and curled up beneath the duvet.

IV

ONE-EYED KING

I had been back in Guangzhou for a fortnight. I was craving a non-urban environment, and to meet Africans who were not hiding from the police or tied to their trading activities. Baiyun Mountain was a good place to meet these liberated types since only people with visa security and a solid financial toehold would frequent such a place of leisure.

The mountain was a breath of fresh air, a forested area a few miles north of the city, and the only high-altitude area in Guangzhou. I took a cable car, which floated just above the canopy and delivered me halfway up the mountain. From a viewing platform, the skyscrapers of Guangzhou were a distant grey blur behind a sea of green vegetation, the kind that once covered the city in pre-industrial times. I then walked along a winding path down through the forest, among the weekend crowds, some of whom stopped to take photos of me.

On my way along the path, I ran into an Igbo man who resembled the British-Nigerian actor Chiwetel Ejiofor and was strolling with his two young half-Chinese sons. He owned a clothes shop at the top of the Tianxiu Building. Business was doing well and his parents-in-law accepted him because he had become a moderately successful businessman.

'They want to know that you are not playing. If you have a house and car, they can see that you are here for your family. Some people, they marry for residency. But others fall in love.'

I asked him about his mixed-race kids. They went to a school where everyone else was full Chinese. Did they suffer?

'Yes,' he replied, without specifying. 'One day people will say to them, "Go to your father". What happens if the Chinese run the world? I won't like it!' he chuckled. Nevertheless, he was quietly optimistic: 'Nobody knew a Black man would become president of the US. Before, they did not give Nigerians residency but now they give. I hope the Chinese can change.'

I continued further down the mountain and chatted briefly to three African men – one from Lesotho, one from Mozambique and the other from Guinea Bissau. The Mozambican talked about the difficulty of learning Chinese. 'There are no tenses and no conjugations,' he said with a strong Portuguese intonation. All three men were studying journalism and planned to return to their home countries to apply their skills there. Now they were travelling around southern China for fun and out of curiosity, to sample the different landscapes. As genuine students on legal visas, they exuded and moved around with a refreshing air of liberty. I wanted to chat with them for longer. By now I was getting fed up with the treadmill of conversation back in Sanyuanli, the shadiness or evasiveness of certain individuals. I must have spoken to at least six dozen people, yet many of these chats were sideways moves that brought me no fresh infor- mation. They often claimed they were in China on unspecified 'business', or they appeared to lie about what they did. Such as the barber Saul who claimed to be a student in Yunnan Province even though he was always in Guangzhou, cutting hair behind a furtively closed curtain. Then there was the pidgin English-speaking Chinese woman at Ikem's jewellery store whose backstory I desperately wanted to learn. I wanted to hear her take on Africans in China but my pleas for substantive conversation were rebuffed with evasive smiles and jokes.

The reasons for keeping a low profile were infinite. So many lost dreams, punctured hopes. Wading into their thoughts and affairs was never going to be easy. I cast my mind back to that bullfrog man who so objected to being photographed by Ikem's son. His anger had seemed tinged with a panic that went beyond a general dislike of being photographed. Most of the people I met were living a regular and honest existence but didn't want to be personally spot-lighted. Being of a similar ethnicity to them granted me a level of access that other Western writers might not have had. Yet that similarity intensified my guilt over our divergent fortunes. I had a passport that smoothed my path around the world. I could dip into these people's lives and then dip out again and return home to London while they remained tethered to a shorter leash. They would confide all sorts on first meeting me but, on figuring out I was a writer, would either clam up or vanish. When Emmanuel, the visa overstayer, happened to walk past me weeks after our conversation, he dropped his smile and averted his gaze.

Part of the reason was the provincial government placing the burden of immigration control on ordinary citizens. Hotels, landlords, employers, educational institutions had to check visas and documents and report anything untoward.

Snitch, or be penalised with a fine. The sense of constant surveillance made Africans wary. And it wasn't just the visa overstayers who were evasive with me but the shipping agents and students too. Those who realised I was asking too many questions rarely confronted me about it. My calls simply went unanswered; scheduled meet-ups were cancelled at the last minute or people simply made no-shows without explanation. One or two of them toyed with me deliberately, which was frustrating and unnerving.

The most aggravating example was a Nigerian pair, Mike and Martin. I met Mike in the lobby of a hotel I was considering moving into in Sanyuanli. It wasn't even me who initiated the conversation. He had turned around to face me at the reception desk and grinned flirtatiously. Dressed in red tracksuit and red Nike trainers, Mike was what's called 'yellow Igbo', i.e. very light-skinned, and he had been bantering with the receptionist in Chinese.

'So you speak Chinese?' I asked.

'Very fucking well,' he grinned. Although middle-aged, he exuded the cockiness of someone twenty years younger. He looked at the camera in my hand and asked if I was going to take a photo of him. I took a few shots. We then sat on a sofa in the lobby and chatted some more. Minutes later, a cold evening wind blew in, prompting us to continue the conversation in his room. I wasn't worried about him assaulting me in any way – my instincts are good like that, and Mike wasn't the type. Still, I got the shock of my life when we entered his pitch-black room and he switched on the light to reveal a bald, fat, dark-skinned man sitting on one of the twin beds, looking at his phone. Why was this person sitting in the dark? And why didn't Mike forewarn me?

'I took the room key,' Mike explained. The fat guy was his friend and roommate, Martin.

'We are more than friends,' Martin said, raising his eyebrows for emphasis. For a minute I thought he meant they were lovers, but he was actually referring to their brotherly bond.

Right from the start, Mike and Martin were savvy about my agenda, and thoroughly uncooperative. They quizzed me on what I was doing in Guangzhou and, through some clever questioning (plus ill-preparation on my part), extracted the truth. I confessed to being a writer, not a tourist or professional photographer.

Both men lived in Yiwu in central Zhejiang Province and said they were in Guangzhou to do some shopping. Everything else about their lives was withheld from me, even their ages. They had met and dodged international 'journalists' like me before, they said, and were only giving me the time of day because I was their 'Naija sista'.

They asked what I thought of Chinese people.

I told them about an incident in my hotel when the maid turned to me and, with a didactic smile, mimed washing herself with a bar of soap.

'She thought I'd never used soap before!' I complained.

Mike chuckled. 'You might be misunderstanding her.'

Martin: 'Some Chinese are stupid. They can insult a Black more than anyone. They are saucy. Very saucy people.'

Slight misuse of the word 'saucy', but I knew what he was getting at. 'What's the alternative explanation?' I asked.

'She was trying to learn you that this is for taking bath.'

'Yes, but why did she need to tell me that?'

'Maybe you don't understand what she was trying to say . . . it might mean so many things.'

'Like what?'

'For example, maybe she just wanted to have a conversation with you. They like foreigners. They want to come to us. They want to make friends with us.'

'A cleaner in a hotel?'

'It doesn't matter . . . the problem is how to communicate. The cleaner is trying to do something to get your attention.'

'You don't have to get angry with the Chinese,' Martin advised. 'They are Third World; even though they are developing, they are still very far in many things. You have not seen something, 'sef. Maybe you went to a restaurant and—' Martin made a hawking and spitting sound. 'What will you do? The same place he's eating. Or maybe you are on a train . . . very nice place—' He made a spitting sound again. 'It's normal to them, but to us it's not.'

'They're friendly, though,' I said.

Martin and Michael nodded. 'I give them seventy per cent,' Martin said. 'In Europe it does not happen like that? They don't respect Blacks?'

I told them that most British racists don't show it in public.

'Why they keep quiet? Is because of the law?' Martin asked.

'Yeah, it's against the law, and they're scared of what white liberals will say.'

We paused to watch the TV. The American tennis player Serena Williams had just lost the final of the Australian Open.

'How old is she now?' Mike pondered. 'Time for her to get married . . . what is she waiting for?'

'The mens are scared of her,' Martin declared. He turned to me. 'Are you married?'

'Nope.'

Mike and Martin were considering spending the evening at Kama nightclub. 'I like Russian girls,' Martin purred.

'The DJ there is my guy,' Mike added. 'He has been here for—' He stopped himself. '—actually, I'm not going to tell you about his story because . . . it is money.'

'Huh?'

'Your story here is all about money. When we read any stories about China then when we find out that it's true story it will make you popular. So what am I going to gain to give you all these secrets?'

I tried not to frown. 'Why are you being so difficult?'

My question drew falsetto titters from the men. 'I'm not trying to be difficult,' Mike replied.

That's when I knew they had no intention of cooperating with me.

It was time to get some food.

We stepped out into the warm night. Bow-legged grandparents with their children and grandchildren strolled about. At a hole-in-the-wall shop, the guys bought me various parts of duck that I had never tried before. The duck's feet were as rubbery and tasteless as I anticipated. Duck liver was OK if rather peppery. The duck neck, on the other hand, was a revelation. Tender and sweet and utterly divine.

Afterwards, Mike and Martin took me to an empty courtyard adjacent to a liquor and grocery store. It was an African hangout that had lost its popularity, they said. In their determination to toy with me, the guys refused to tell me its name or why it had fallen from grace. I contained my anger as we sat at some outdoor tables and ordered Nigerian stew and rice. The food was delivered by a Chinese courier. There were only two other tables in the courtyard. On one table sat a quartet of francophone men, listening to Congolese music on an iPad. The other table was occupied by tipsy Nigerians who exchanged insults with the Chinese storekeeper, a young guy in skinny jeans and a shiny blazer with the collar upturned. He screamed at the Nigerians in Mandarin spiced with occasional English: 'Come now . . . come close, mother-fucker!' The Nigerians roared back in a mix of Igbo and English. All I caught were the words 'your government' and 'fuck you'. Neither side understood the other's language. Bravado and aggression were the only things being communicated, yet they stopped short of any violence, mainly because the Chinese guy needed the Nigerians' custom and they needed his merchandise. *Pax economica*.

Mike and Martin continued to evade my questions, taunting me about all the juicy anecdotes they could give me. Later on, they were joined by a friend and his 'wife'. She didn't breathe a word, just sat there in stony silence for an hour. I suspect she was actually a prostitute. The men taunted me some more, and Martin said he would give me information if I 'made Mike happy'. This allusion to sexual favours was designed to press my buttons. And it worked.

I hailed a taxi and said goodbye.

—

'Have you picked up any Chinese?' I asked a Sierra Leonean man I got chatting to on the street one afternoon.

'I have tried to talk to women,' he responded, 'but I have not found anybody. I am a born again Christian. I'm trying not to fornicate.'

I had actually been enquiring about his language skills, but he got the wrong end of the stick. But since we were now on the subject I asked the man how long he thought he could remain celibate. He suppressed a smile: 'For as long as I am here.'

The women shortage seemed to me one of the more unfortunate aspects of life for African men living in China. This hustler's life in China – so unpredictable and precarious, and without a time limit – was better suited to the male biological clock. Most of the women I encountered were business owners on short buying trips. Few of them lived here permanently. The ones who did, I was informed, were often wives of men who ran successful long-established businesses and lived in the suburbs, or they were prostitutes. For obvious reasons, I never met a man who confessed to using one.

One Igbo Nigerian man, Dennis, described my situation as an outnumbered female thus: 'In my village they would say that in a city of blind people, anyone with one eye is the king. When you meet an Igbo woman abroad, especially like this, it seems like she is the talk of the town because you are happy to see her . . . I pray I will find a Nigerian wife.'

There was no competition when a woman comes along, he said, because the men were 'industrious' and 'here to make money'. He would rather wait and pray he'll find a Nigerian wife than date a Chinese woman and subject himself to discrimination and suspicion from her kinfolk.

Another guy, Stanley, dated Chinese girls but they weren't his preference.

'Let me be honest to you, you understand? I told you I came to China in 2010. I can't tell you I haven't had sex. If I tell you like that, I'm lying to you.' A short, stocky Mike Tyson lookalike, albeit gentle and sweet, Stanley exported furniture to Nigeria. 'Chinese girls . . . one problem with them is that their mentality and yours is not the same. It's very easy – you can get them. But the way they think . . . a Chinese girl, you can have sex with her one, two, three, four, five times in one night, they will not be OK . . . they will say they need more. You tell her you are tired and she says, how can you be tired? Their men eat too much sugar, they are not strong. The girls like Black dick. You understand what I mean? And our people . . . you know we are strong. So they don't enjoy their people. Anyone who sleeps with a Black man, they will never want to sleep with their people again.'

I had heard this self-aggrandisement conflated with social analysis many times before. Guys like Stanley will reject every ridiculous Black stereotype except this one. Russian girls were expensive dates, he claimed ('They have to stay in bar all the time. It's not our life.') He gently begged and cajoled me to date him, tried to philosophise his way into my bed, presenting our union as some kind of mathematical logic ('I'm a man, you're a woman'). It was amusing but also sad. He refused to go back to Nigeria until he became 'rich' so that his wife and kids would not suffer like he did. And he also rejected the idea of marrying someone and leaving her in Nigeria. He had seen this happen to a friend who lived apart from his wife for ten years. 'You cannot expect a woman to not have sex all that time. Meanwhile you are enjoying yourself, going to clubs. If she go and sleep with someone I would not blame her. Because she's a human being. She has feelings.'

Some men treated me as if I were a prostitute. They never

mentioned the word itself but it was apparent in their presumptuousness. Like the evening in Sanyuanli when I was walking out of a market complex and a Nigerian voice called out from behind me: 'I like your structure.'

I turned around and found a man with a toothpick wedged between his teeth sizing up my figure. He came at me with a sway-shouldered swagger, but instead of stopping to talk some more he walked right past me and continued down the street. Something about him demanded that I follow. Hesitantly.

'Are you Nigerian?' The man said this with his head facing forward, his voice projecting into the crowd ahead, as he peacocked along.

'Are you talking to me?' I asked.

'Yes, now. Let's go.' He motioned forwards with a startling confidence. I was irritated by his assumption that as a woman I was amenable and available to him, though, of course, my trotting after him was doing nothing to disabuse him of that notion.

His name was Steve. His dark, craggy skin looked roughened by hardship and appeared to have aged him beyond his forty-something years. Steve led me to a Nigerian restaurant adjacent to a dark courtyard where trains screeched overhead. A giant flat-screen TV had been mounted on the restaurant's exterior wall. We sat at a courtyard table with two other men, neither of whom told me their names or asked for mine. One of them sported massive biceps, wore a sleeveless puffer jacket, a chunky gold watch and had three mobile phones piled up next to his plate. The top phone was gold-plated. The man neither greeted me nor spoke to me. He simply bellowed to the others in Igbo. His voice was a diabolical rasp, deep and laryngeal and unbelievably loud. For much of the time the others listened to him in silence.

The other of Steve's friends asked only if I wanted a drink. When I responded that I already had water, he said: 'I did not ask you about water. Do you want drink? Beer?'

His gruffness was startling.

The waitress was Chinese and the wife of the Biceps Man who, I discovered, owned the restaurant. She had the mannerisms of a certain archetypal kind of dissatisfied Nigerian woman who moves around in a slow, seething saunter. Her pouty lips might have cracked had she deigned to smile.

'How are you, my sista?' she said, pen and pad in hand, ready to take my order.

She brought me jollof rice that she had cooked herself. It was delicious. The Chinese can copy everything, even Nigerian cuisine.

I watched a Nigerian music video on the TV screen. The singer was dancing around a woman in hot pants, waving his arms hip-hop style. The men still weren't talking to me, they just barked with each other.

What was I doing here?

Steve still had that toothpick in his mouth. He wasn't eating, just dancing a little in his seat. Though he never smiled or talked to me properly there was playfulness beneath the deadpan surface, a happiness that came from hot antic-ipation. At one point he clutched the underside of my knee beneath the table. I pushed his hand away.

'Did I make mistake?' he said.

'Yes. You can't just touch a woman like that. You need permission first.'

'Can I take permission?'

'No.'

I turned to the TV screen. In the second music video, a Nigerian singer stepped out of a private jet; he wore a tuxedo and pulled out some diamonds stored in the front of his pants.

Every few minutes the restaurant boss would rise from the table and walk to the corner of the courtyard to talk quietly to a variety of young men carrying satchels. Were they drug dealers?

I got up to leave.

'Sit down, we are going together now,' Steve said. 'Where is your hotel?'

I shook my head and left.

—

Steve's thirst for female company spoke of the overwhelming gender imbalance among Africans in Guangzhou. Women – the kind that were young, unmarried and not focused on short-term trading missions – were few and far between, which is why the guys often spoke in glowing terms about Kama nightclub. It was a particularly fun place to meet women. So fun, it brought a smile to the lips of most who mentioned its name. By all accounts Kama drew a flashy, international crowd of Arab, African and Eastern European men, and Russian and Colombian 'girls'. A place, I had been told, that I should experience at least once. The online reviews – written in fittingly ropey English – offered a taste of what I could expect. A certain 'Mohamed from Iran' wrote:

I had the experience of Kama club in Guangzhou for fifth time . . . If you are looking for columbian ladies to pick up, here is an excellent place that you are looking for. It's unbeatable in terms of atmosphere and beautiful ladies.

This joint sounded deliciously flashy, the perfect place for a bad-taste safari.

My alarm clock went off at least two hours after I had fallen asleep. I was at an age where late-night clubbing wasn't the fun end to an evening but rather the ungodly start of a new day. Dragging myself out of bed, I put on some clothes and hailed a taxi to Kama Club where things were only beginning.

I arrived after midnight, wearing jeans and Nike trainers, unwilling to sacrifice comfort for style (not that I even owned a mini skirt or shiny dress). A very tall and confident Chinese man in a black-and-white striped suit welcomed me in. I descended a flight of neon-green steps and emerged into a dark space, half-filled almost entirely with men. This was not what I was expecting. I sat on a stool at the back and cast a censorious eye over the scene.

Behind the DJ a huge screen displayed a ticker tape message: 'Prostitution and whoring are prohibited . . .' False virtues are screamed out the loudest, although on this night they really meant it. Guangzhou was having one of its occasional one-week-only crackdowns on prostitution.

Arabic men in sweaters sat at tables. I guess nobody had forewarned them about the hooker ban. They sipped drinks, smoked shisha pipes, scratched their silvery five o'clock shadows and stared ahead wordlessly, occasionally breaking their silence to crack a joke or take selfies on their phones. There were Chinese men maintaining a similarly anticipatory pose. Puerto Rican cumbia music and Egyptian hip hop thumped from the speakers; disco ceiling lights swirled around the clientele, casting derisive shadows on their lifelessness.

In my naivety, I had assumed that in a place known for prostitutes, there would still be 'normal' women enjoying an evening out. This prostitution ban exposed the fact that Kama Club was in essence a brothel with a dancefloor attached.

The only excitement came from a table occupied by a group of friends that was genuine and mixed-gender and celebrating someone's birthday. A balding Arab in a knitted top wielded a cigarette and waved his arms, nineties rave-style, to the Arabic Happy Birthday song. A waiter handed him a birthday cake. Chinese security guards patrolled the floor like school examiners, the black of their jackets offset with red arm sashes. They sauntered past a trio of Southeast Asian women who were twiddling their earrings in silence. One of them eyed me sitting alone at my table. Bet she was wondering what I was doing there.

Every man who walked past me did a double take. Prostitutes here were generally Eastern European, Asian or Colombian – not African, and certainly not wearing jeans and trainers. As I sat alone, I began to worry that onlookers would mistake me for an ageing hooker with fuck-me-not shoes and a poor understanding of her customer base. Minutes later a white guy made eye contact and sauntered towards me. I was ready to give him a huffy knock back (I'm a respectable woman!), but then I thought perhaps my presence, in all its mystery and discordance, had aroused his curiosity. The man bent down, put his face close to my ear and hollered in a Slavic accent: 'You got party pills?'

Relief and indignation hit me both at once. Curiosity didn't exist in this milieu – there was a box for everyone, and I was the African drug dealer.

A while later, a group of six young African men entered the club and sat at a table next to mine. This was more my 'market', even if they were all young enough to call me Aunty. How long could I sit there alone without being questioned or propositioned? What response would I give? Once again, I was worrying about nothing – the boys paid me no attention whatsoever. They surveyed me and the insipid scene, then shuffled out within minutes of arriving.

Just as I was getting bored, the lights and music stopped abruptly and plunged the place into substantial darkness. The security guards motioned for everyone to get out. It was just after 3 a.m.

Outside, as I waited with a few others for a taxi, an Arab man with a bouffant coiffure came over. 'Hello, I want to talk to you. What is your name?' I was his last-gasp attempt at a piece of ass, even if it wasn't in heels and a dress.

'Sorry,' I told him, 'I have to go.' I climbed into a taxi.

V

SCAPEGOATS

I thought about Martin and Mike and their fondness for Kama Club, and I was reminded of their evasiveness that evening. It still frustrated me. In order to understand part of the reason why Africans in Guangzhou were cagey and kept a low profile, and why they were treated with disdain by the police, one must go back to an important event that happened in 2009, just across the street from Ikem's shop.

At 2 p.m. on July 15, he and his friend Chinedu watched from the window as plain-clothed policemen, launching a raid to round up Africans for imprisonment and deportation, swept into the Tangqi Foreign Trade Clothes Plaza building. The Africans weren't sure whether these policemen were real or just local troublemakers. Guangzhou has two types of police: the regular force, and then Chengguan officers from the Urban Administrative and Law Enforcement Bureau. These guys regularly stop and search Africans. Some of them are part-timers and not professionally trained; a rag-tag force known for misusing their authority, harassing the poor and small-time vendors. When the officers burst into the Tangqi building, the visa overstayers panicked and fled as the Chinese chased them around the building and out onto the street.

Emmanuel Egisimba, a Nigerian clothes trader, and another man surnamed Ndubuisi, were pursued into a nearby building. They scrambled to the second floor, opened a window and jumped out. According to official reports, Egisimba suffered a cut to his head and was bleeding when he jumped from the Tangqi building. Ikem told me that one man's intestines were exposed. The protesters carried the wounded men to the police station, situated diagonally opposite, and lay them there. 'Go on, eat them!' they raged sarcastically. Egisimba was taken to hospital but later died.

Subsequently, two hundred African men gathered on the street in impromptu protest against police persecution of Black people. It caused traffic chaos. The Chinese authorities' response to the protest wasn't heavy-handed, partly because they knew some of the protesters and partly because they wanted to avoid an escalation. They simply captured the protesters' faces on CCTV and later denied visa extensions to all those identified as troublemakers.

But from that point on, things changed. Africans in Guangzhou kept a lower profile and became more wary of the police – and wary of talking to journalists and writers like me.

—

Several years on, the quotidian calm of Sanyuanli's streets seemed a world away from the unrest of the Tangqi building incident. While walking along the street, I stopped to chat to a man getting a haircut on the pavement opposite Canaan Market. George was his name. Tall, Nigerian, bearded, perhaps in his early thirties, he sat with his strong arms folded across his chest as hair clippings tumbled onto his shoulders. It turned out that he had a theory about the root causes of Nigerians' unsavoury image in Guangzhou, which stretched back to around 2008.

George's voice rose above the thundering traffic and bore a faint American cadence, and his vocabulary suggested he was more educated than average. He told me that he now taught English in Hunan Province but used to live in Sanyuanli.

'Basically, if you ask guys who've lived here long enough they'll tell you there was a time when people were fighting out here. With knives, here on this street.' George pointed at the ground beneath him.

'Why?' I asked.

'Some of them belonged to a cult called the Apapa,' George said. In Nigeria, 'cults' began life as student groups in universities (similar to American fraternities and sororities) that became involved in violence and organized crime. It started in the 1980s when the military regime used these cults to subdue student unions and any faculty members agitating for democracy. Within a decade some of these groups evolved into mafia-style gangs that spread their tentacles internationally. 'Other guys said they belonged to a secret cult,' George said. 'And these are guys that didn't even fucking go to school. Then they came up to China and started initiating all these guys who knew nothing and shit. They started fighting each other.'

Gang colours became an issue.

'I was walking down the street one day, and some guys asked me, "Hey, why are you putting on a black shirt?" I'm thinking, what the fuck? It's my shirt. And he asked me if I belonged to his cult. I said no. He said, "Then you shouldn't put it on." It was hilarious,' George laughed indignantly. 'But I knew this guy could squeeze me because he's a big, hefty guy, you know? And I said, "OK, but it's my shirt." They've done a lot of things here, I'm telling you. Crazy.'

A second man chimed in. 'That's why they don't like us. Because here a man was butchered. He was a drug mule.'

'Butchered by other Nigerians?' I asked.

The man nodded in the affirmative. 'Mmmm-hmmm. Because he couldn't excrete all the cocaine.'

'Are the guys who caused all the trouble still around here?' I asked George.

'They're in the slammer. Some of them were deported but it's a ripple effect. It goes on and on. The problem is with the management of the country. We used to own all the shops here,' George swept his hand across the parade in front of us. But getting visas became difficult.

'Most of these guys came for business but decided to stay. Some came purposefully just to stay. They made no preparation for what they were going to do when they came to China. Nothing. There was a time when people would stand here and ask me for money: "I never chop, give me money." And some of them would come up to you as though they put the money in your pocket! "Give me this." This place has cooled down a lot, I'm telling you. So that's why they don't like us. It's not that they don't like Nigerians but . . .' George sighed, kissed his teeth and paused. 'Look, I'm sorry to say this, but most of the Nigerians here are Igbo.'

George was an Esan from southern Nigeria. When I told him about Ikem's hopes of becoming Biafran as a way of improving his image amongst the Chinese, George was sceptical about the Chinese ever recognising such a situation.

'They wouldn't do that. You know why? Because they have territories that want to secede. Xinjiang and places like that.' For decades China has suppressed separatist movements in Xinjiang, an ethnic Uighur Muslim province in the northwest, and in Tibet in its southwest, as part of its mission to keep these distinctly non-Han cultures within the People's Republic. While Beijing allegedly runs internment camps in Xinjiang and imprisons monks in Tibet, it keeps its gunships pointed at Taiwan, still considered a 'renegade province'. Meanwhile, Hong Kong jitters at the erosion of free speech and democracy under Chinese rule, which was not supposed to start in earnest until 2047. Pro-democracy lawmakers in Hong Kong have been arrested. With a track record like this, there was no reason why the Chinese government would distinguish between Nigerian ethnicities or approve of any secession from that country.

I was momentarily distracted by the shouts of a cantankerous Chinese granny selling a pile of cheap trainers with the help of her tween-age grandson. She kept slapping him around the head when not shouting at customers who dared to barter.

A third Nigerian man told me that though he hadn't returned home in eight years, he preferred life in Nigeria because of the precarious visa situation in China. He hadn't warmed to the locals either.

'I hate them the same way they hate me. They don't love me so why should I love them? I come to China but I don't have Chinese friends. I'm here to do business. That's why we have to go home and apply what we know to that place.'

But it is difficult to apply knowledge to a country where electricity blackouts can momentarily darken entire airports and roads are cleaved by sludgy ditches; where chemistry graduates vie with semi-literate labourers for jobs; where the government doesn't strive to deliver per capita growth; where cancer patients have to go abroad for treatment.

George explained that the media put pressure on the local government because there were so many journalists asking questions at the police station and the immigration office. The authorities did not welcome the media attention.

'Whenever something happens the high-level government makes a call to the low-level government. "What's going on? Why is there something wrong?" So when Africans come to the street to demand freedom in 2009, that was very symbolic. All the information about the African community in Guangdong becomes sensitive.

'No more photos, no more talking to local officials. The government wanted to diminish the presence of Africans. Downplay it. The Guangzhou local government pushed many Africans out to neighbouring cities. It's no longer Guangzhou's problem. They used every opportunity to achieve this aim. Crackdowns on fake goods, tax. The house rental system – in the beginning there were no inspections . . . But later you needed to report, you needed to submit your information to the local police. If you stay with a friend at their house, they now have to register you with the local police. If you give your space to a friend for free, it's a problem.'

—

The main street near Taojin subway station was alive with neon and modernity. Restaurants with laminated menus whose names didn't just exist in people's heads but shone smartly on the exterior; coffee shops dotted with the Apple-shaped lights of laptops, and internationally recognised clothing outlets. It all brought into sharp relief the relative dowdiness of Sanyuanli, which had registered only in my deeper consciousness but had been weighing me down subliminally. Coming to the upwardly mobile parts of Guangzhou always lifted a cloud.

The sun had gone down, and on the pavement outside a McDonald's stood a Black man, looking from side to side at the shoppers strolling by. The satchel on his shoulder and his watchful, lingering glances marked him out as a drug dealer.

Although only 8 p.m., he plied his trade openly. His body formed a silhouette against the yellow lights of the restaurant. So conspicuous yet so dark and invisible, he was a black-man-shaped hole in this society. I had been informed that the police often turn a blind eye to petty African drug dealing so long as they sell to Africans only. If true, it is an interestingly bespoke application of law based on ethnicity and nationality. This 'othering' of immigrants was a signal, if any more were needed, that China has no long-term intention of integrating Africans into its society.

When I asked the occasional English-speaking Chinese person what they thought of Africans they usually admitted to having little or no interaction with them. 'They are known for doing drugs,' was a common response. The virtues of the African law-abiding majority were frustratingly – and by definition – invisible. The humble, blameless existence doesn't make it into the newspapers or on to YouTube. The drug-dealer stereotype, though not remotely representative of the community, is rooted, like most stereotypes, in partial truth. But Africans aren't the only ones doing it. Nor do they do it on a large scale. If only I could speak Mandarin, I would beat the brows of Chinese bigots with a few facts and reminders.

When it comes to drug crimes the British set an inglorious and far grander precedent in the nineteenth century. Correcting the trade imbalance with China is a conundrum that has afflicted all countries in the world for centuries. In the nineteenth century the British were buying Chinese tea and other products; but the Chinese, who were masters of manufacturing, had no demand for British goods. Desperate to correct the trade imbalance, the UK government realised the only way to stimulate Chinese demand for their stuff was to supply something addictive: opium. The Brits began manufacturing and selling the narcotic in what was perhaps the world's greatest act of state-sponsored drug dealing. After cultivating the poppies in the fields of their then-colony Bengal, the British sold the drug to a Chinese population keen to consume a product they believed could aid sexual performance. Soon China under the Qing dynasty was awash with opium dens in which skeletal addicts flopped listlessly in hazes of smoke. On seeing the carnage wreaked upon his society, the emperor tried to block sales by the British. It led to a series of battles known as the Opium Wars, which took place between 1839 and 1860. The British won, and subsequently obtained territorial concessions from the Chinese, including Hong Kong Island for ninety-nine years.

Decades later, in 1997, the world watched as Hong Kong's last British governor, Chris Patten, set sail from Victoria

Harbour for the last time. Donning a feathered pith helmet, and backed by the glittering skyscraper skyline, Patten's departure was the culmination of imperial drug pushing that had been successfully laundered through time into capitalist success, pomp, splendour and a sense of moral superiority.

Where the British left off, others took over. Chinese drug dealers had occupied Guangzhou's Sanyuanli district long before Africans settled there. The geography of urban crime often remains the same in cities, the only thing changing is the ethnic composition. Current drug dealing isn't peculiar to Nigerians, either. The academic Shanshan Lan points out that Southeast Asians, Middle Easterners and overseas Chinese are all involved in narcotics-related crimes in Guangzhou. Africans, she says, are singled out and scapegoated more often because of their visibility, but in reality none of these groups could carry out their operations without collusion with local Chinese mafia gangs (a big problem in Guangdong Province), corrupt local police and Chinese-run underground banks. In a province-wide bust in 2015, the police seized more than five tons of drugs and arrested 5,000 Chinese people suspected of drug-related crimes.

The British did what they needed to do when they hit the great wall of Chinese self-sufficiency. And if the world's largest empire and the Chinese could descend into drug dealing, then why not Africans? Many of them are innocents forced by circumstance down the wrong path. Life as a trader is ridden with surprise sinkholes. Too often they fall victim to scammers and thieving airport or customs officers back home, or are sold dud products by unscrupulous Chinese wholesalers who know that they can't extend their visas and sort out the problem. Traders who have overstayed their visas can't call the police.

'Many people spent a lot of money to come here in 2006 to 2008,' said Ikem during another of my visits to his shop. Some visa overstayers never intend to come to China in the first place, he said. Their travel agents inform them they're heading for Japan, Korea and Malaysia only to send them to China instead. Some of these folk are left stranded with zero knowledge of Asian geography, wandering the streets asking for directions to 'Japan'.

'They're stuck here. There's nowhere from here to anywhere. With other passports you can go to Malaysia, et cetera, but when you are coming on a Nigerian passport you are going nowhere. So they stay here, they survive, they marry. And maybe there's a woman here who becomes your girlfriend. The only way to survive . . . there's no job, there's no money. The girl will be taking care of you for little things. The person based here will be tripped up and in debt. That's why he cannot eat or pay his rent. That's when he starts doing bad things to make money. It is very difficult when you see somebody with that level of life here. Very difficult. Because they do not have a comfortable home to stay.

'I can't blame them because some people . . . their mothers die because they don't have 10,000 naira for the medication. And she dies, you know? It's terrible. And you know that if they get caught, they are going to die or go to jail. Many of them are there in the prison. They do not want to tell us what that place looks like. It is hell.'

By some accounts, Chinese prisons involve cheek-by-jowl sleeping, communal hole-in-the-ground toilets; hours of manual labour accompanied by kicks and beatings; and measly food rations consisting of white rice, potatoes and water, which are a recipe for stomach bugs and diabetes. Hundreds of Africans languish on death row in countries across East Asia for drug offences, I was told.

Even when it is financially possible for these guys to return to Nigeria, macho pride sometimes prevents them from doing so. Igbo culture demands that men make a success of themselves and look after their wives and families. Some overstayers would rather die in China than show their face back home with less than US$50,000 in savings.

I shook my head at the futility of patriarchy.

—

The only drug dealer who talked to me openly was a man called Frederick. I met him while having lunch in a Nigerian restaurant. A short man in his forties, Frederick was light-skinned with a moustache, and wore a facial expression that was as cheeky as the 'I Love Weed' embossed on his baseball cap.

'So what do you do here?' I asked him.

He smiled coyly. 'Business.'

That old chestnut.

'What kind of business?'

He smiled again. It didn't take him long to admit he was a drug dealer. His candour came as a surprise. At first I thought he was lying to impress, but he stood to gain nothing from lying. He said he had a fake French passport and had spent two years in prison in Switzerland on drug charges. That's why he had now shifted operations to China.

I have always been curious about informal trade networks, particularly the illegitimate ones. My world is one of formal qualifications and applications and resumés. The workings of informality were a mystery to me. How does one move to a country you know very little about and establish links with the underworld? How do you pick out such people and develop mutual trust?

'Use your "Number Six",' he said, pointing at his brain. It was about watching people, asking indirect questions. 'My mother used to tell me, "He who asks questions is not lost." You must think intelligently.' Fred looked me up and down. 'I think you are the same. I can see it in the way you are. You are moving around here, asking questions . . .'

Frederick didn't know I was a writer. Luckily he mistook my curiosity as an ambition to enter the drug trade. He could get me into the business if I wished, he said.

'Even if I wanted to I wouldn't,' I replied. 'Don't you worry about what your mother or father will think?' I asked.

He shrugged.

'You're very confident.'

He smiled. 'I am a second God.'

'What do you mean?'

'God made man in his image.' This was the first of Fred's many twistings of the Scripture.

'Don't you worry that God will punish you for what you do?' I asked.

He shook his head slowly, and with an intense stare, said, 'John chapter three, verse sixteen says, "For God so loved the world that he gave his one and only Son, that whoever believes in him shall not perish but have eternal life." We

are all sinners. Jesus did not die for those righteous people—'
Fred pointed to himself. 'He died for us sinners.'

I cackled. It was the most self-serving interpretation of
the Bible ever. 'So you are fine with what you do?'

Fred nodded, chewing on his toothpick.

Like almost everyone else in that restaurant, Fred was
Igbo. I asked him why so many of the traders in Guangzhou
were from that ethnic group. I knew what was coming – yet
another statement of ethnic chauvinism.

'Yoruba men don't like to hustle,' he smiled.

VI

NORTHERN EXPOSURE

I wanted to head to the north of the country, to the ancient town of Pingyao. Getting there involved going to Changsha and then flying to the nearest big city, Taiyuan, in the northern province of Shanxi. For the first three hours of the bus journey to Changsha I drifted in and out of sleep, my eyes occasionally opening to Hunan Province's mountains and green fields, and to China's transformation from the agrarian to the industrial.

There were sprawling and massive industrial parks, and a solitary buffalo standing in a small field amongst residential houses. A farmer carrying pails attached to a pole across his shoulders walked along in a field, a huge power plant rising behind him. I glimpsed a shop selling a white effigy of Chairman Mao, born in this province in 1893 to a poor farmer who later became wealthy. Though the political and economic legacy of 'The Great Helmsman' was everywhere, this was the first Mao paraphernalia I had seen since arriving in China.

Towards nightfall, I arrived in Changsha. I hadn't known this city existed until I realised I needed to fly from it. I assumed it would be as small and provincial as Zhangjiajie, but I was wrong: the streets were wide and sparkled with neon. Skyscrapers glittered, and there were Apple stores, high-end boutique shops and gleaming cars everywhere. It looked like Las Vegas, the kind of city I should have heard of. Via a Google search I learned that Changsha has a population of 7 million, which is not much smaller than London. How had this place skipped my radar? Megacities are supposed to be cosmopolitan centres of global commerce, born of ancient history, fed by empire and international trade. Yet modern-day Changsha has sprouted without any of those characteristics.

China is full of Changshas. Between the late 1970s and late 1990s, government reforms allowed local governments to develop land in order to accommodate the hundreds of millions of farmers migrating to the cities. In the last twenty years the country has constructed more than 400 cities with populations of at least one million – the equivalent of building the urban mass of Western Europe.

Even the Chinese themselves were shocked at the transformation. I remember a conversation I had with Patricia, a friend from my boarding school days. She grew up in Hong Kong and hadn't been to the mainland in decades. When I told Pat that I had visited Panyu, a neighbourhood in Guangzhou popular with Western expats, she gasped: 'I used to visit my grandmother there when I was a child. It was nothing but farms and chickens!'

I felt the reverse shock: having never experienced China prior to 2016 I couldn't envisage Panyu as being farmland within my lifetime. It put Nigeria's population problems into perspective. Our biggest city, Lagos, with its 20-million population and shantytowns that expand endlessly over land

and into the sea, suddenly seemed quite small and potentially manageable.

—

The next morning I boarded a flight to Taiyuan. Seated next to me was a sweet teenage girl who insisted on chatting despite the language barrier. We communicated via her phone's translation app. She was from Taiyuan, she told me, and had just taken an exam in Changsha. She then taught me how to correctly pronounce my ultimate destination, Pingyao ('Peenyaw'). How anyone travelled in China prior to the invention of smartphones is beyond me. Even my own pre-internet travels in francophone countries seemed impossibly challenging from today's perspective, as if my cognitive functioning were vastly superior back then.

On the approach to landing in Taiyuan, I looked down on farming terraces and folds of beautiful mountains. Buildings were arranged in tidy quadrants, and even the small settlements were organised in neat rows in a nod to communist central planning. It got me thinking about China's centralised bureaucracy versus Africa's less organised governance. Each had its pros and cons. Nigerian politicians often used chaos as an instrument of control and wealth accumulation. The bureaucratic organisation required to implement full-blown Soviet- or Chinese-style communism is absent. But this slapdash approach also – ironically – undermines any attempts by Islamic terrorists, for example, to organise in a truly systematic way. China's tight organisation has also led to a vice grip on terrorism, speedy urban development and effective control of the SARS pandemic in 2002–4, but it also enabled it to roll out Mao's Cultural Revolution to devastating effect. I'm not sure which is preferable.

On the ground, Taiyuan's wide boulevards contained the occasional Mao statue. The architecture was communist, gargantuan and grey: stick-a-brick skyscrapers and monolithic edifices enlivened only by the curlicue dragon statues flanking their entrances. Stuck without wifi, I mimed my way to an intercity bus thanks to some helpful strangers. Just before my coach departed for Pingyao, the on-board TV monitor broadcast a safety video designed to put the shits up anyone thinking about not putting on a seatbelt. Horrified, I watched footage of accidents captured by on-board cameras – passengers being slung across the bus, slamming against the ceiling or flying out of the windows.

I put on my seatbelt immediately.

The bus rolled towards Pingyao. The town lies in central Shanxi Province (450 miles southwest of Beijing), and is renowned for its well-preserved city walls and architecture, one of the few surviving examples of an ancient Chinese town. Mao destroyed many similar cities during the Cultural Revolution. That, combined with Deng Xiaoping's economic reforms had eroded much of the old China. I wanted to experience this shrinking heritage.

Enjoying Pingyao's ancient beauty required schlepping through the torpor of the Shanxi countryside first. Shanxi Province is China's historical coal-mining region. One quarter of the country's coal and one third of the world's carbon emissions originate here. The industry is Victorian in its filth and working conditions. Soot-faced miners live right next to coal-fired power plants, and each year the black earth swallows up several people in landslides. Although I was nowhere near a coalmine, the coal dust hung in the air and its particles were visible in the sunrays. The sore throat and nasty cough I eventually developed were the worst of my life. This, I had to concede, was my carbon footprint karma: all those smartphones, those international flights, the plastic packaging . . .

The national government is trying to wean itself off coal and use more eco-friendly technology. It has put China in the unusual position of being home to the world's dark satanic mills while also leading the way in green technology.

My bus trundled along through small towns, emptied by the New Year holidays. We passed one-storey factories and leafless trees, acre upon acre of brown fields and farms, dotted occasionally by flocks of sheep and frozen rivers; warehouses and cranes and light industry.

This mix of the industrial and agricultural called to mind a painting by Yang Yongliang I once saw. At first sight it looks like a black and white traditional *shan shui* ('mountain water') painting, with undulating hills in a rural, bygone landscape. But zoom in and you realise that Yang has super-imposed a 3D digital collage of densely packed Shanghai skyscrapers and cranes onto the mountains so that the urban skyline mirrors the rural topography, creating a blend of old and modern, urban and rural.

Things outside my window seemed so large-scale, passing by in quantities I had never seen before: electricity pylons strung along for miles; row upon row of greenhouses; fields of sapling spruces that spread over hundreds of acres; a cargo train seemingly the length of Belgium chugging in the distance. And in a building, forty-odd chefs in white hats occupying the entire length of the second floor.

Then, out of nowhere towards late afternoon, rising majestically from the horizon, were tall, thick, sloping walls topped with elegant turrets with barbican gates. It took my breath away.

Pingyao. The ancient city.

Pingyao dates back 2,700 years and was a financial centre of China during the Qing dynasty. This was China in all its architectural glory: upturned eaves, tiny carvings lined along the rooftops; lacquered storefronts, courtyards and stone dragon carvings sitting at the bottom of bannister rails. Pingyao has retained its original layout, with the *bagua* ('eight areas') pattern. There are almost 4,000 preserved homes, and the streets and storefronts still largely look as they did in ancient times.

Next morning I stepped out onto Pingyao's main drag. Its 50,000 residents were swamped by thousands of domestic tourists and a handful of foreigners like me. A lady held out a selfie stick and forced her reluctant son – by grabbing his chin and lifting his face upwards – to pose with her. The main streets were cluttered with so much tourist tat, so many food stalls, that Pingyao was almost unrecognisable as a functioning town.

Beeping motorised rickshaws, scarves, baseball caps with communist red-star insignia and kitsch imperial hats with pigtails attached. Pingyao is an architectural husk devoured from within by tourism. A part of me questioned the point of it all. But whenever I looked at the architecture, those gorgeous curly roofs, it confirmed my belief that aesthetics are everything. What further authenticity would I want anyhow? Did I actually *want* to taste Pingyao's ancient food? Or watch its residents practising ancient hygiene standards?

Or to experience ancient attitudes towards me as a Black person?

Pingyao was lucky to have survived Mao's Cultural Revolution. Beginning in 1966, his student-led Red Guards ran a somewhat inconsistent campaign to destroy pre-communist elements of Chinese culture, known as the 'Four Olds': Old Ideas, Old Customs, Old Culture and Old Habits. Confucius's cemetery was attacked; intellectuals were publicly humiliated; Chinese literature and religious symbols and temples were desecrated or destroyed, along with ancient bronze vessels, jade carvings, rare manuscripts, paintings, ceramics and calligraphic works – anything associated with imperialism.

China and Nigeria were similar in their adeptness at destroying their artistic heritages in the 1970s. China did it through systematic and deliberate vandalism under Mao; Nigeria did it through casual dereliction. Different causes, similar outcomes. Now the Chinese are reclaiming and cele-brating their heritage, buying it back from Europe since the year 2000, especially as their own markets were filled with forgeries. Nigerians too are challenging the historical theft of artefacts, for example the famous Benin Bronzes, many of which were stolen during a punitive raid by the British in 1897 and kept in various museums around Europe. Following a recent campaign for restitution, certain institu-tions, such as Cambridge University and Berlin's Ethnologisches Museum, have agreed to return these sculp-tures to Nigeria.

—

I ate dinner alone in a Pingyao restaurant – noodles and pork and vegetables. On a nearby table a group of middle-aged and elderly people twisted their necks to watch me eat. Intrigued smiles. Under normal circumstances I can use chopsticks without a glitch. Doing so in front of a grinning audience of the people who invented the things was a different matter. My fingers turned into palsied claws, and a chunk of pork fell back onto my plate. In hindsight I should have eaten the Chinese way, i.e. lowered my face towards my bowl and shovelled the food into my mouth. But I kept forgetting I was in a place where that was socially acceptable.

The restaurant manager offered me a bowl of what seemed like custard and water. 'On the house,' he said in very broken English. The soup was delicious. There was nobody to tell me exactly what it was. The manager watched me genially. He wanted to chat with me as much as I wanted to chat with him. I hadn't had a meaningful conversation with a Chinese person since arriving in the country, save for passing encounters with a few English-speakers in Guangzhou.

The chatter around me was distinctly different from that in Guangzhou. I hadn't appreciated the number and variety of dialects and accents in China. We foreigners are more accustomed to hearing Putonghua, i.e. standard Mandarin, or the Cantonese spoken by much of the diaspora. The people of Pingyao and their Jin dialect spoke with an accent that sounded thoroughly alien and, to my ignorant ears, not very Chinese. I was stunned to hear sounds similar to those made by Cornish people in western England ('ooh arr').

I wanted to speak Mandarin. In the several weeks I had been in the country I had learned only a handful of words. My ignorance of the language was becoming a problem now that I was going deeper into the interior. The iPhone and Google images were my crutch for everything, my mouthpiece and my brain. Without wifi or access to a VPN I had the communication skills of a dog (which, though effective at times, were never nuanced enough). I resolved to learn a few Mandarin phrases.

But my Chinese pronunciation was a real problem when it came to ordering tea: each time I demanded 'cha' nobody understood me. I tested every conceivable intonation only to have the waitresses come back with plain hot water. Requesting lǜchá (green tea) was even trickier, the 'lǜ' part of the word requiring an almost cunnilingual waggling of the tongue.

For dinner on my final evening in Pingyao I picked a restaurant along the central main road. The waitress, a portly, no-nonsense madam, showed me the wall-mounted photos of food and stood close by me as I decided what to eat. I could feel her eyes boring into my profile. Feeling pressured, I hastily selected a salty beef in soup and noodles, which I regretted when it arrived.

The written menu was no clearer because it was written in Chinese English or Chinglish, where Chinese is translated into nonsensical English. I'll never understand what algorithm produces this gibberish but it is thoroughly and endlessly entertaining. No traveller returns from China without a stack of hilarious Chinglish menu dishes, each one as unique as a snowflake. My favourites:

'Dog Comes Next'
'The west lake beef infarction'
'My cousin element six Treasure'
'Three cups ginger groping'
'Everything has'
'The emperor burn shrimp sauce on the planet'.

VII

IT'S A SEX PROBLEM

I was back in Sanyuanli again.

Not far from Canaan Market was a shoe market with racks of ladies' shoes at the entrance. A quartet of African men picked up some ladies' wedges and inspected them while deep in conversation with one another. The incongruence of macho-looking men eyeing up and handling feminine footwear was comical.

'Do you know which shoes women like?' I asked.

'Yes. I know,' one man nodded. 'They don't want anything with a high heel.'

'Who are you buying them for?'

'These are for girls who are still at school.'

Deji was his name. Clean-cut, smooth-skinned and skinny, Deji was a student at a university in Yunnan Province, studying for a degree in tourism and hospitality. His shy and bespectacled friend, Toyin, was an aeronautical engineering undergraduate. The boys were the latest in a tradition of Africans studying in China since the mid-1950s as part of Mao's mission to create solidarity among 'Third World' countries. The term 'Third World' emerged during the Cold

War to describe countries that remained non-aligned with either NATO or the Warsaw Pact. It was initially a political description rather than an economic one. By the late 1980s, more than 2,000 Africans were studying in China. Nowadays, there are that many studying in Guangdong Province alone, most of them on Chinese government scholarships.

Deji was learning about hospitality.

'The five-star hotels in China . . . the services aren't five-star, maybe four-star, three-star. They don't know how to handle five-star services, so most of the time they franchise. They own the building, then they just buy the name, Sheraton, etc. So five-star services in China aren't good. Only in Shanghai and Beijing the services are good because they employ foreigners.'

I asked Deji why Nigerians don't do hotels so well.

'Because Nigerians, we are so arrogant. If someone is rich in Nigeria he is arrogant. They don't care. And the government does not favour the hospitality industry. There are no standard hotel policies. But in China they have people who monitor five-star hotels. There are Chinese government organisations that monitor the five-star hotels. They come every week and check the kitchens. You can't cook nonsense. You can never get food poisoning.

'Most Nigerians who study in China, it's very difficult for them to go back home because: number one – to get a job is very, very difficult. And you're going to have a boss who will boss you around and he doesn't understand quality and everything you've learned.' Deji kissed his teeth in frustration. 'You're just going to waste your knowledge and you don't have a say, because they will sack you the next day. But here, you can contribute. Like when I was doing my internship – you can contribute and say, "No, no, no, this is how you do it", and they listen to me. I'm just an intern, but they listen. And they jot it down and work on it. But in Nigeria they don't care. They tell you, "Who are you?"

'At the university, my teachers all have PhDs, they know what they're doing. They travel abroad and they go to tourism sites. They visited hotels abroad.'

'Will you go back?' I asked Toyin. He and Deji laughed at the suggestion. 'No, I don't think so. I've been in China for, like, six years now. I came to stay for one month and I've been here since.'

Deji had returned to the motherland twice, but said he can't stay there. 'It's very, very difficult to be in Nigeria.'

'People don't care,' Toyin added. 'The corruption has really eaten into our hearts.'

At that moment, a man rode past on his bicycle and hawked up phlegm with loud relish and lobbed it on the floor. I recoiled. Deji chuckled: 'That's what you see in China.'

I asked how easy it will be for them to get jobs.

Deji sighed. 'The ratio is like ten of us out of one hundred. Among us Africans, it's even more difficult. Nigerians here can't open bank account, can't get visa. People have to work in import-export.'

Some African students already start to work before graduation. They skip classes and use their language skills to translate for compatriot merchants attending the Canton Trade Fair. In the 1990s, a number of these African students even migrated from their university locations to Guangzhou after graduating. Some of them became very successful, community leaders and local celebrities, stalwarts of the

African–Chinese community. But not all graduates enjoy such a happy outcome.

'So your prospects of getting a job are better in Nigeria?' I asked Deji.

'Yes. You can stay here for fifty years and you will never get citizenship,' Toyin said. 'The Chinese government they don't want too much influx of foreigners, and they don't really like Blacks. If you don't flash them your UK passport, they say, "Oh, Africa? Go away, go, go, go!"'

It was odd that he was getting qualifications in a country where he couldn't live and practise his skills and training, only to return to a country where the smaller, less ambitious, hotel market could scupper his hopes of running a three-star boutique hotel.

After our conversation ended, I explained to Deji that I was writing a book and that I wanted more insights about life for African students here. He agreed to meet me again a few days later. But when the day came he made an excuse about collecting a friend from the airport. I never saw or heard from him again.

Months later I came across a book that gave the most candid source of information about student life in China, at least in the 1960s. It was written by a Ghanaian man called Emmanuel John Hevi, who was one of thousands of African students attending Chinese universities during the days of Mao. Granting scholarships to Africans was China's way of exercising soft power during the Cold War and winning the hearts and minds of developing countries.

Hevi, who became secretary general of the African students' union, wrote a deliciously scathing account of his time as a student in Beijing in the early sixties, in a book called *An African Student in China*. It is said that the winners write history, but sometimes the most disgruntled can be the most vocal too.

According to Hevi, many African students heading to China either knew nothing about the country or perceived it as a socialist paradise. Hevi says his feelings were neutral. China was neither bogeyman nor saviour, he says, but by the time he left in 1962 the scales had tipped. He wrote his book to let readers know what communist China was 'really like' and to warn Ghana's first post-independence leadership not to follow in Mao's socialist footsteps.

Hevi pours his scorn from a great height. He begins with the blue Zhongshan suits everyone had to wear under Mao's communist rule. What is this 'colour fetish?' he asks. He shudders at the possibility that Africans might one day adopt it and abandon the 'gay and multi-coloured clothes that make any African country a place to remember'.

The Zhongshan suits may have symbolised belonging and equality, but in varsity China equality took a backseat where living standards were concerned. Hevi says the Chinese government was keen to impress its guest students, so – in a rare case of African privilege – it gave African students preferential treatment over their local counterparts (a concept known as *waishi*). While Chinese students were packed eight in a room, foreigners luxuriated one or two to a room. Their generous stipends were even higher than the Chinese tutors' salaries. Chinese students were fed smelly cabbage while African students received the choicest foods (relatively speaking). The Africans wore better clothes and enjoyed longer holidays while their Chinese counterparts laboured resentfully in fields and factories.

Safe to say none of this endeared the African students to the local Chinese populace. But the Africans had no choice. The authorities specifically instructed them to jump to the front of queues at bus stops. Sometimes Hevi and his friends were so embarrassed by the privilege foisted upon them they chose to stick to their place in line. Still, the locals' subsequent hostility came as no surprise to Hevi. He sympathised with them. The Chinese were good people, he believed, but because they worked so hard for so little, communism had turned them into 'veritable dragons'.

Hevi wasn't happy with the indoctrination either. Marxist doctrine was top of the agenda, even in language lessons. The vocabulary learned was almost entirely political, no conversational stuff:

> 'The whole world will certainly develop in the direction of communism; this is a law of social evolution.'
> 'One can never speak enough of the Party's goodness.'
> 'I shall never forget what the Party has told me.'
> 'The Party calls upon all youth to study Chairman Mao's works and to become good students of Chairman Mao.'

'I found myself begging one of our tutors to tell me how to say "water" in Chinese,' Hevi writes. Translation dictionaries weren't available in those days. The Africans pressured the university to introduce textbooks with a broader vocabulary. The authorities eventually relented. But imbibing Marxist doctrine still came at the exclusion of everything else (including each student's chosen field of study). Hevi lost interest in his studies and resorted to doing the bare minimum to pass his exams.

This 'undesirable political indoctrination', he believed, went against the official objective of learning and benefiting their home countries after their studies.

Hevi's political scepticism and honesty won him no favours among his Chinese tutors. When asked why Chinese people sympathise with the liberation struggles of the oppressed peoples of the world, he replied that it was because the Chinese had themselves been oppressed. His tutors loved that portion of his response, of course. But then came the second part: he declared that the Chinese sympathised with oppressed peoples of the world only because they 'wanted to win markets', particularly in Africa. His Chinese tutors bridled at his 'heretical' ideas. Nonetheless, those ideas proved prescient – Deng Xiaoping introduced his free-market reforms the following decade.

African students were not as in love with Chinese communism as the Beijing government had hoped, and weren't so willing to be indoctrinated. Hevi claims their Chinese hosts consequently felt the students were biting the hand that had fed them.

Although conditions for African students were preferable to those of their Chinese classmates, some of them still found life in China unbearable. The small stipends, bad food, limited entertainment options, poor medical treatment (aspirin administered for every ailment) and the 'Black-Yellow mutual hostility' compelled certain students to go on strike or return home. Protests ensued, followed by an exodus in 1961. The Zanzibari students upped and left. So too did students from outside Africa, such as the Cubans and Yemenis. Somali students went on hunger strike over poor conditions, Hevi says. These protests terrified the

Chinese government who feared they would set a worrying example to the general population of China. Nearly all of the Cameroonian students were expelled in 1962.

For those who stayed, student social life offered little exciting distraction. Cinema options were restricted to Chinese movies that fixated on the Revolution or the Korean War and seemed to end in more or less the same way: a dying, wounded soldier or another soldier streaking across the screen waving a red flag. Hevi was gagging for a bit of Hollywood or sci-fi – anything vaguely imaginative. He and other foreign students stopped bothering to attend these film sessions.

The Africans were keen to make friends with the Chinese but found it quite difficult. The few Chinese friends they had were foisted upon them by the university, so the Africans ended up in segregated groups. The few non-foisted Chinese friends turned out to be informers (the Chinese idiom: *géqiángyǒu'ěr*, which means 'the walls have ears', was especially apposite here). These informants reported on what books they read, the conversations they had, the people they met: in other words, gauging their loyalty to the communist project. All other Chinese students were warned not to associate with the foreigners, so the 'friendly' overtures – once sussed out – irritated Hevi. The constant surveillance, he says, was a mental strain.

The Chinese authorities' concerns about fraternising with foreigners weren't just political, however. There was one issue that exposed the lie of developing-world brotherhood, the one issue that never fails to separate the ideological wheat from the chaff; a concern too frivolous and taboo to express out loud yet so existentially urgent and fundamental: sex.

Interracial dating was an unintended consequence of the preferential treatment given to African students over Chinese ones. Male African students were a catch in the eyes of some Chinese female students, who were as forthcoming as the African boys in 'crossing the line'.

Hevi recalls campus dance parties where the DJ banged out the same three tunes, 'poor Soviet imitations' snappily titled 'Socialism Is Good' and suchlike. Chinese guys could dance with African women without a problem, but vice versa was a different story. Hevi recalls that every time an African man danced with a Chinese woman, a tutor or Youth League activist would watch them from the sidelines until the song was over, then scuttle up to the girl demanding to know what she and her dance partner had been talking about. Either the girl confessed to 'unsanctioned fraternisations' or she could be 'criticised', i.e. given a punishment ranging from incarceration to hard labour in the communes. Simply being seen with a Black guy was cause enough for some Chinese girls to be punished. Some Africans preferred to stop seeing Chinese girls altogether rather than risk getting them in trouble, according to Hevi. However, the more determined interracial couples began meeting on the down-low in public parks. It was still risky, what with the Africans' high-visibility skin, but in matters of sex no mountain is too high.

The reaction to interracial dating proved that the Chinese government (as opposed to the general population, Hevi stresses) were not self-styled defenders of Africans and other persecuted peoples but plain old racists. Their 'calculated invocations of brotherhood' didn't match the reality, and the preferential treatment given to foreigners was purely for long-term Chinese gain. Believe it or not, it was racial sexual tension on campus that ultimately mutated and evolved (or at least fed) into the Tiananmen Square protest and massacre of 1989.

The Nanjing anti-African protests were mass demonstrations and riots against African students in Nanjing. Male Chinese students would watch in envy as their female counterparts sauntered over to the African buildings (an Italian friend of mine who studied in Beijing in 1991 recalls the Chinese girls being very proactive in pursuing African male students in that era). Being foreigners, the Africans wore better clothes, carried bigger wads of stipend cash in their fancy denim pockets, and had cushier rooms for roll-arounds between the sheets. Of course, many of them were considered attractive in their own right, but these material advantages had long had Chinese boys simmering, and the interracial sex heated their sentiments to boiling point.

Open animosity towards African students began in the late 1970s and intensified in the 1980s. In 1979, male Chinese students at the Shanghai Textile Engineering Institute attacked their African counterparts with makeshift weapons, accusing them of playing 'loud' music and making sexual remarks towards Chinese women. In 1980, Chinese students at various Nanjing universities hung up posters complaining about the government lavishing food and clothing on African visitors. Five years later, a Chinese woman who spent time in an African student's dorm room could be arrested for doing so.

Clashes between Chinese and African male students grew more frequent and sometimes led to the arrest and deportation of the Black students. Mob violence of this sort recurred throughout the 1980s. The government or police did not do enough to protect the foreign students. Instead, Black students were being deported to such an extent that some African ambassadors advised their governments to send fewer students to China.

The anti-African protests staged at Nanjing's Hohai University in 1988–89 were the biggest of them all. After months of escalating tensions between African and Chinese students, the latter staged mass demonstrations that lasted from December 1988 until the following January. In 1988 in an attempt to prevent interracial liaisons, the university authorities had built a wall dubbed 'The Great Wall' around the foreign students' hall. The university president said the structure was necessary 'to prevent a small number of African students from bringing women to their rooms . . . it's a sex problem,' he proclaimed.

African students responded by knocking down the wall. In retaliation, the university deducted the repair work from their stipends. The Black students protested against this move. Fast forward to Christmas Eve that year. A dance event on campus. The university demanded that all foreigners register their guests at the university gate. When two African students arrived, accompanied by Chinese women, a brawl ensued. Some reports say the security guard suspected the women were prostitutes. There were also rumours that a Chinese woman had been kidnapped. In any case, more than 300 male Chinese students gathered around the foreign students' sleeping quarters and set fire to the Africans' dormitories. Police reined in the Chinese aggressors while many of the Africans fled to the train stations, hoping to find sanctuary in their respective embassies, but they were prevented by the authorities from boarding the trains in order to be questioned.

By this time, a mob of 3,000 Chinese students were singing

the national anthem and chanting, 'Down with the Black devils!' They called for the government to prosecute the Africans and to stop giving foreign students more rights than the Chinese. The following evening the marchers, holding banners, converged on the railway station and called for human rights and political reform. It took riot police several days to pacify them all.

Within a week, three of the African students had been deported. The others returned to their universities where they were placed under night curfews. All meet-ups with their Chinese girlfriends were restricted to the lounge area.

Anti-African demonstrations spread to other cities, including Shanghai and Beijing. The agitation merged with anti-government sentiments, which culminated in the Tiananmen Square protests four months later in April 1989. Thousands of people gathered in the square, clambering onto statues, linking arms, chanting for change and holding placards. There, mixed in among the 'Absolute Power Corrupts Absolutely' banners, were slogans that screamed 'Stop Taking Advantage of Chinese Women'.

—

Late one night I watched a Chinese cookery programme on TV. I was enjoying watching the chef chopping up vegetables but then the camera suddenly cut to him slamming a turtle onto a chopping board and hacking it into pieces before tossing the chunks into a sizzling wok. I shuddered. For all my globetrotting, some foreign customs could still rock me to the core.

Sometimes the culture shock was not so much shocking

as puzzling. I once tuned into the Chinese state television broadcaster, CCTV, and watched a subtitled documentary about a mountaineering enthusiast who insisted on dragging his two-year-old daughter with him on his adventures. Barely a scene went by without the poor girl crying. Fastened to her daddy's back, the child bawled as he climbed mountainous rock faces, lashed by rain and wind. She was car sick along an isolated road, yet the man kept going in the belief that exposure to these experiences was vital for her personal development.

Later in the film, the father and his friend – also a mountaineer – were in conversation at a restaurant. Family is the most important thing, they confirmed to one another, although each saw fault in the other's parenting style. The second mountaineer, a renowned climber in China, politely suggested that Mountaineer One wait until his daughter turn six before bringing her on his adventures. I applauded his good sense and compassion until he himself revealed his own bizarre parenting practices. His teenage son, he complained, 'lacked courage'. Apparently the boy had asked him for the latest iPad. Mountaineer Two said he would grant his son's request on condition that he 'slap one of his classmates'. The boy refused because he felt that slapping another person was wrong. Dad was disgusted. Courage, he told the teenager, was the ability to step beyond your boundaries and comfort zone; it was about breaking the rules. Now it was Mountaineer One's turn to maintain a diplomatic silence.

I found it all fascinating and faintly comical. Weird as the conversation seemed, it was the first time I had observed a conversation between two Chinese people that I could understand, thanks to the subtitles. Whether they were representative of their society I didn't know, but there was an intimacy to the portrayal of those mountaineers. It got me wondering about the Chinese media and whether it gave an equally involved portrayal of the Black people living amongst them. Given that few Chinese citizens had actually met and interacted with 'black ghosts', the media had a huge influence on how they perceived them. Judging by the stories that emerged, the coverage was at best unsophisticated, and at worst racist in the most retrogressive way.

There was the notorious TV commercial for a Chinese laundry detergent brand that made headlines around the world after it depicted a Black man being shoved into a washing machine and then emerging as a pristine Chinese man. There was also the infamous photo exhibition at the Hubei Provincial Museum in Wuhan, in which images of African people were framed alongside animals that had similar facial expressions. This section of the exhibition was titled '相由心生', which loosely translates as 'outward appearance follows inner reality'. The photographer, Yu Huiping, said he wanted to give visitors a sense of 'prim-itive life' in Africa, and show the harmony of humans, animals and nature. In each photo frame an African face was juxtaposed with animals, many of them primates. The most offensive was a chimp that was baring its teeth and held its mouth agape, next to a young boy whose mouth was also open. The boy's gape was neither a scream nor a yawn – there was an air of contrivance to it, as if he had been instructed to shape his mouth that way, like a patient in a dentist's chair. Some of the other photos juxtaposed people with non-primates, but I suspect that these frames were mere smokescreens to conceal the ape photo and its implicit message.

I came across a photo of the photographer himself on a website. He is on location in Africa in his all-in-one camouflage suit, looking every bit the parody of a photographer in 'Wildest Aaafricaah'. It turns out that he was part of a collective of photographers who took these photos for the museum exhibition.

When the photos became public, a Zimbabwean woman called Samantha Sibanda, a Beijing-based activist, educator and general firecracker, was having none of it. A founder of the city's Pride of Africa Asia Awards, Sibanda launched a petition on social media to get the photos taken down. It was a success, but when the photographers and museum withheld apologies, Sibanda got on a flight to Wuhan to meet them face to face and explain why the photos were so unacceptable.

The meeting lasted two tense days; two days of huffing and defensive puffing from the photographers, who explained to Sibanda that the exhibit wasn't meant to be offensive but was an artistic work inspired by the animals of the Chinese zodiac. A Chinese person juxtaposed with a panda would be a compliment, they said, because the bears are held in high regard. The photographers also claimed they were planning on doing the same thing for kids in a poor village in China in order to raise funds for them.

Sibanda told the Beijinger website: 'I thought to myself: "My God! These people will never get it." She came close to quitting but reminded herself, 'Sam, you're an educator, and you have to educate these people. Because if you don't try, and just dismiss them as racist, Africans in China will always lament it, and will always say "Oh! If only they knew better." So I'll tell you where I come from, and by the end of the conversation you will know.'

By the end she reportedly reduced some of the photographers to tears as they issued a written apology and pledged to portray Africa in a more nuanced and positive light.

Most evidence of Chinese perceptions about Africa are based on these visual representations, but we only hear about the negative ones (and the visual ones at that) because they attract international media attention in a way that positive, anodyne ones do not. I wondered if the real picture was more nuanced. What did Chinese literature or internet forums have to say about Africans? The only detailed analysis I could lay my hands on was a book, *Mapping the New African Diaspora in China*, written and researched by anthropologist Shanshan Lan.

She says that in 2006, a survey by *China Youth Daily* showed that 70 per cent of Chinese knew little or nothing about Africa, and about 42 per cent got their information about the continent from the news, films, internet or newspapers. The internet often focuses on Black sexuality or debates about Chinese aid to Africa. Concerns about immigration diluting the 'purity' of the Chinese race are occasionally peppered with complimentary and broad-minded comments, often from traders who have direct experiences with Africans. The general prejudice is overlaid with an overarching government message of friendly Sino-African relations in which racism does not officially exist in China.

Dr Lan collected data from popular Chinese web forums Sina.com and Tianyashequ (Tianya Club). The latter had 85 million registered users by 2013. She searched the phrase

'Guangzhou heiren' (Blacks in Guangzhou) and selected 3,000 web posts from the twenty-two most viewed discussion threads between 2007 and 2013. Five major themes cropped up: the Black threat; xenophobia; Han chauvinism; criticism of national immigration policy; and 'learning from Western examples'. The researchers identified two counternarratives: the Sino-African friendship discourse, and stories of Chinese wives of Nigerian men.

'Within the black threat discourse, we identify five interrelated themes: Afro-phobia, dehumanisation, hypersexuality, criminalisation, and low *suzhi*.* Together they construct a negative image of blacks as racially inferior to Chinese and socially undesirable as foreign migrants.'

In Shan's analysis, terms like 'black devil' came up 569 times; 'trash' 119 times; 'ox' appeared fifteen times; 'low IQ' thirteen times; 'poisonous tumour' made ten appearances, followed by 'beast', 'inferior race', 'chimpanzees' and 'cancer'. The Chinese looked favourably on Africans who assimilate into Chinese culture, providing, it seems, they don't ripple the gene pool.

A famous example is the singer Emmanuel Uwechue (stage names Hao Ge and Hao Di) who performs traditional Chinese songs. Back in 2010, the world became fascinated by the sight of this Black man singing in that sentimental Chinese style, accompanied by mawkish, weeping orchestras. It was the polar opposite of African music: slow, no polyrhythms, minimal body movement and slightly less vocal exuberance. Hao Ge has told Western media that he has ambitions beyond this current genre (he admitted feeling a little trapped within it),

---

* 'Suzhi', 'quality' or 'human quality', is a term that describes a person's behaviour, education, ethics and ambition. It is related to the concepts of 'breeding' (*jiaoyang* 教养) and 'personal cultivation' or refinement (*xiuyang* 修养).

which may explain why he ends certain songs with a soulful, American-style coda. It then appears that he changed his stage name to Hao Di and, for reasons unknown, claimed this 'new' singer was his brother. Hao Di embraced the political aspect of music with kowtowing fervour. He is known for singing patriotic songs with titles such as 'Without the Communist Party There Would Be No New China'. Whether or not one likes his music, it is hard not to be impressed by his command of Mandarin. His voice is beautiful too.

I once showed a YouTube video of Hao Ge's performance to my Chinese American friend, Deborah. She's a laidback, mild-mannered sort. However, the sight of Hao Ge dressed in the long, silky traditional changshan suit triggered an uncharacteristic rage in her. Deborah ranted about how the Communist Party split up families, sent people into forced labour, and trashed thousands of years of books and beautiful historical artefacts. Seeing a Nigerian man singing the party's praises was more than she could take. Some Chinese diasporans have a hatred of the Communist Party that I'm too detached to share. How, she fumed, could the party that crushed pre-communist traditions now celebrate a man dressed in clothing it once reviled as 'bourgeois'?

She ordered me to switch off the video.

—

In which century did Africans first arrive in China? Historically, Guangzhou is used to influxes of foreigners. Its location on the Pearl River delta made it the terminal for the maritime Silk Road and a trading port for centuries. The Moroccan traveller Ibn Battuta visited in the fourteenth century, followed later by, among others, Japanese pirates and British, Scandinavian and Armenian merchants. The remains of a seventh-century mosque still stand in the city.

Africans were known to be living in Guangzhou as far back as the eleventh century, and contact between the two peoples goes back even further. Africans came to China during the Tang dynasty in 618–907 CE, and possibly earlier, along a sea route between Dar es Salaam in Tanzania and China. An excavation from the Shang dynasty (1600–1046 BC) at Anyang in Henan Province found a skull of negroid appearance. Many negroid images, sculptures and carvings were found in this prefecture, but they may actually be Melanesian, Negrito or even Persian. Nobody is sure.

The earliest indication of Black people in China appears to be in wooden tablet documents from the Han dynasty (206 BC–220 CE) known as 'Juyan'. Sixty of these tablets recorded the identity of soldiers, including their rank, age, height and skin colour. Fifty-three individuals were described as 'black', and another as 'yellow black'. The Juyan Hanjian tablets indicate that quite a few Blacks in the Chinese army became officials and border officers. Sixteen were of noble rank.

Some scholars dispute the definition of 'black'. However, hundreds of thousands of foreigners were living in the Hexi Corridor of Gansu Province in the north, with the records stating that they were a similar height to Nilotic East Africans, who were presumably taller than the Han Chinese of the era. Ethiopia and the Egyptian city of Alexandria are mentioned in the *Shiji* ('Records of the Grand Historian'), which was compiled by Sima Quian during the Han dynasty in the late second to early first century BC.

During the prosperous days of the Tang dynasty and Song dynasty, cosmopolitan cities such as Chang'an, Guangzhou and Quanzhou attracted many foreigners. They came as diplomats, officials, visitors, traders, workers, artists, musicians, acrobats and animal trainers. Black people also appear to have joined the retinue of royal families and even the emperor, as evidenced in a fourteenth-century painting in the Asian Art Museum in San Francisco, which depicts a Black official in high-rank clothing. The thirteenth-century artist Liu Guangdao also has a painting, 'Yuan Shizu chulie tu' ('Kublai Khan Hunting'), showing the emperor and empress with two attendants, one of whom is Black and riding a horse alongside them.

In Dunhuang, northwest China, there are hundreds of Buddhist Tang-era cave paintings containing black-skinned figures. Lady Pei's tomb in Xi'an contains a Black pottery figure. The 15cm figure has muscles, red lips, curly hair, a high and wide nose and the big white eyes of Zanzibar people as described by Marco Polo. Still, some argue that these were not Africans but Asian Negritos, i.e. the indigenous population of Southeast Asia, who are short with wide noses, curly hair and dark skin. Most of them were absorbed by lighter-skinned Austroasiatic and Austronesian groups that migrated from Southeast Asia in Neolithic times, but some isolated Negrito groups still exist today, such as the Semang peoples of Malaysia.

Another example of the Africa-China link is the qilin, a mythical equine animal in ancient China, which appeared in a stone sculpture in the Han dynasty. It looks like a cross between a dragon and a horse and was probably influenced by the giraffes brought to one Ming emperor in the fifteenth century from a voyage to the coast of modern-day Somalia.

Prior to the sixteenth century, researcher Zhouchang Ai argues, Blacks were mostly sent – not sold – by Persians, Arabs or Javanese to Chinese authorities. During the Atlantic slave trade, Europeans brought Africans to China. The British and French had African servants in coastal China, and when the Dutch invaded Taiwan during the Ming period, Black people were among the Dutch and Chinese armies. The Portuguese enlisted Africans as sailors and soldiers for two centuries, including one hundred men to help them repel Dutch attacks on the Portuguese colony of Macao in 1622. Around that time the English merchant trader and traveller Peter Mundy wrote about two 'Abyssinians' (Ethiopians) who had escaped the Portuguese and went on to become Cantonese interpreters. When the Chinese army captured more than sixty soldiers in battle, an Ethiopian and a Sudanese were among the captives.

Records show that the Portuguese took ivory, tortoise shells and rhino horn from East Africa to China, along with African women who were forced to become concubines. These Africans, like others in the Indian Ocean world, spoke languages in addition to their own. Swahili, with its Bantu grammar and sprinkling of Arabic words, served as a lingua franca for many enslaved Africans who were held in East Africa or crossed the Indian Ocean.

The historical evidence of Africans in pre-modern China may be ambiguous in parts, but it seems a fair bet that they have been in the Middle Kingdom for centuries, making their various contributions before dissolving like drops of ink in a swimming pool.

VIII

CHUNGKING MANSIONS

Ageing skyscrapers soar from the waters of Victoria Harbour, their topography almost matching that of the verdant hills undulating behind them. The Bank of China Tower with the iconic criss-cross pattern rises above its neighbouring skyscrapers like a plant seeking light in a forest. Middle England corporate Joneses in suits trundle along the walkways of Central train stations as if worm-holed straight from London Waterloo.

Hong Kong.

Gone are the junks that once traversed the harbour. Productivity no longer bustles in quite the same way as before. It is digitised, silent, less tangible. What was once the gateway to China is now a cool respite from the mainland, a way of touching base with the UK and savouring the freedom before Chinese rule comes into full effect. Beijing culture looms already: Hong Kong movie-makers now make their films in Mandarin rather than Cantonese in order to satisfy the mainland market. But Hong Kong still feels like a British outpost, less frenetic than the mainland, and I was very happy to be here. I had come to renew my visa and explore the city's African community. Since British laws still apply, Africans can obtain residence permits and work visas in Hong Kong more easily than in mainland China.

I headed to the Chungking Mansions, a famous (and infamous) cluster of tower blocks near Victoria Harbour in the district of Tsim Sha Tsui, where many Africans either live or come to socialise. Chungking appears with little advance notice. The road leading up to it is a canyon of concrete skyscrapers cluttered with billboards and neon, Chow Tai Fook jewellers and Louis Vuitton shops; where Hong Kong old-timers brush disdainfully past their newly moneyed compatriots from the mainland. Somewhere between a Rolex shop and an upmarket hotel, Chungking is suddenly visible, a tall structure in the late-fifties composite building style battered by decades of tropical rains.

On the steps at the entrance, a dozen stubbly Indian men representing hotels inside the building stood in clusters and pestered pedestrians with incessant offers of accommodation. I sidestepped them and entered. The change of atmosphere was sudden and powerful. A bazaar of electronic items; kitsch paintings; Filipina women exchanging currency behind windows ringed with neon; stalls selling Indian and Chinese food, manned mostly by Southeast Asian men on behalf of their Chinese landlords. Their womenfolk were nowhere to be seen. It was a mini Kolkata, hot and humid, and the smell of chicken biryani masked the bouquet of dewy masculinity.

Entrepreneurs from Asia, sub-Saharan Africa and other regions come here to buy goods and sell them back home – in 2008, 20 per cent of all phones used in sub-Saharan Africa passed through Chungking Mansions, before Guangzhou overtook it as a wholesale centre.

Almost 130 nationalities live within Chungking's seventeen-storey walls. In this Tower of Babel are graduates; entrepreneurs; asylum seekers; scammers; artists; drug dealers and users; entrepreneurs-turned-addicts; Western backpackers who can't afford anywhere else in the city and occasionally baulk on encountering the African-run hotels; Nepalese heroin addicts; sex workers from various countries; Filipina and Indonesian maids on their days off. In many ways, Chungking is the ultimate manifestation of capitalism's free movement of people, labour, money and goods.

Illegal immigrants are known to run from the police, who give chase if and when they can be bothered to do the accompanying paperwork. They play hide and seek amongst Chungking's warren of rooms and stairwells, which are carpeted in bird shit.

I took an instant liking to Chungking. I loved its compactness and heterogeneity. The doors on each floor are like portals that lead into miniature cultural universes. On the third floor, the elevators open and spit you out in little India, where restaurants with names like the Delhi Club blast curry-flavoured air into the hotel rooms upstairs through weeping air conditioners. On another floor, behind another door, you suddenly find yourself in 'Nigeria', with tiny restaurants the size of a triple hotel room, serving yam and okra soup.

Towards the back of the ground floor was a cluster of African clothes shops and makeshift bars. There I met a chunky, dark-skinned Ghanaian man with a beautiful, dimpled smile.

'If you ask an African whether they have been to Hong Kong and they tell you yes, then you ask them, "Have you been to Chungking Mansions?"' he told me. Edwin was his name. 'If they say no, then they have not been to Hong Kong. It's a lie!' he laughed.

Exactly how does someone with no contacts in China come to a place like this and go about creating a life for themselves?

'Honestly, I did not know anyone here. I just have this travelling experience. So when I arrived the first thing I did was I went to the ticket station, and I asked them, "I want to go where there are a lot of foreigners, especially Africans." So the man was like, "Tsim Sha Tsui, Chungking Mansion". This very building!' Edwin laughed. 'If foreigner steals from you, just wait here every day and you will find him! Because if you don't come here you won't find your own country food. I like this place.

'So when I arrived they said, "Go to TST, take bus number E23." Honestly, I came here with two hundred dollars. Can you imagine that? You just trust God, pray. The moment we got to TST, I saw a lot of foreigners. Oh my! I walked into this Chungking Mansions. It was 2004. I stood here. From morning until two o'clock in the afternoon I didn't find any Black people here. They start coming in the night. They were avoiding police checks, which normally occur during the day. I stood here for a long time. I saw one guy. He told me there were many Ghanaians here. I told him hello. His name is Kojo. Kojo is all of us our father.'

Edwin's eyes lit up at the mention of Kojo. He worked at one of the Chinese-run hotels in Chungking. Since the bosses weren't there, Kojo let Edwin sleep on the hotel floor by the reception desk. In the mornings Edwin helped clean the hotel. Then at lunchtime, when the Chinese boss arrived, he would hide in a space further down the corridor. Kojo gave him free food.

'I want to tell you something stupid . . . how we survive,' Edwin said with a coy grin. 'So Kojo said to me, "Is your penis working?" I said, "What do you mean? Why do you ask me this question?" Kojo said, "I want to know." I said, "Yes, my penis is working." He said, "Because if your penis is not working, don't even bother to live here. Just book your return ticket and go back home because you are not going to survive in this country. Chinese men and women will not give you even a free gift of one dollar. There's nothing like 'giving' here. And if your dick is working then you can fuck their women and when you fuck a woman they'll give you anything you want. Some of your problem they will solve it for you. Once they have you they are gone, totally. Because they have never had the experience . . . ever."'

Edwin re-enacted his shock. 'I'm a Christian. My ma is a pastor back home. We are not taught to be sleeping around. The pastors who arrived here, to survive they fuck like hell!' Edwin cackled. 'They drop everything down. Then the women they start to support you, small small.

'I got married. The marriage wasn't really from my heart but I had no choice.' Edwin wanted to get residency in Hong Kong. 'The Chinese and African culture are totally different. We couldn't blend together. So after five years she filed for a divorce. We didn't fight. We didn't have any problems. But it was the parents. The parents cannot accept us, that's the problem.'

'Did you meet her parents?' I asked.

'Of course. But they reject you.'

'How do they reject you?'

'They say we Africans, we sleep on the tree. That mentality is on their mind. They'll give you food, they'll give you everything. But when you sit with them and you begin to learn the language very well and you can hear their conversation . . .' He grimaced. 'Oh my god!'

'What were they saying?'

'They say things like, "These guys, you know they don't love you, they are only here for residence and after they have their residence they are going to divorce you and go marry their people. Be very careful, they are thieves. They are not trustworthy." My ex-wife's mother was like, "You have to be careful of people because in their country they practise polygamy. And they will have a wife back home." I didn't have *any* wife back home. The thing is that they watch these things on the TV. It wasn't easy.'

Edwin went on to study interior design at a university in Hong Kong. Design was his passion, although he was confined to a job in transport. He showed me photos of African-style furniture he saved from the internet. He was inspired by Chinese furniture. I told him I loved Kumasi carpentry. He liked Ghanaian furniture but wanted to 'take it to a higher level', put it on 3D moulding. He said Chinese furniture looks great but the quality is unreliable. Despite being a frustrated designer, Edwin enjoyed his life. He went on holidays to the Philippines and Thailand. 'When a Thai fry chicken for you, you will not want to eat African chicken again. They fry it crispy.'

Edwin and his friends weren't enamoured by Chinese-style meat preparation – the steaming of meat, especially fish. It was 'undercooked' and made him want to puke. 'You can't chew the bone. Africans will never get SARS,' Edwin said in reference to the avian flu that swept across Asia in 2003, 'because we boil our meat very well.'

Would African food ever take off in China?

Edwin shook his head. 'We cannot market our food, it's too heavy. You put eba on the table. Who wants to eat eba?' (*Eba* or *gari* is a Nigerian staple food based on cassava flour.) 'My ex-wife and I have a son, he is nine years old. I know Ghana food is good and that gari is healthy and strong, but when one time I give this boy eba in the morning, within a few minutes he was gone. *Asleep!*' Edwin flopped forward. 'This food is more than sleeping tablet. The food is *heavy*. You understand what I'm saying? But when he eats salad and things, he is fine. We need to stop eating so much gari. It's not helping us. We have to do something about African food. Our food is not presentable. Indian food is everywhere. Ghanaian, African food is not.'

I mention that the Chinese in London and the US modify their food to suit foreign palates. Perhaps we should do the same?

'We are advancing, but it's too slow.'

A man ambled towards Edwin. Hands in his pockets, he had an aimless, lacklustre look about him. Edwin shook his hand. 'Found anything yet?' The guy shook his head and smiled faintly, then sauntered off again. 'He's here illegally,' Edwin explained. 'We are trying to find work for him.'

—

While walking on the street outside the Mansions, I locked eyes with a good-looking man standing on the pavement with a couple of his friends. I knew he wasn't one to brush off, and my instincts proved correct. CJ was a breath of fresh air. Tall, well dressed, with sunglasses propped on his head, he was a prosperous Igbo exporter of goods to Nigeria, and he exuded the calmness and satisfaction of a man in charge of his affairs. Hong Kong had been good to him, and he needed and wanted nothing from me other than chilled-out conversation. We had a beer in a tiny Nigerian restaurant on the fourth floor of Chungking Mansions.

CJ had started off small, doing groupage shipping (sharing a cargo box with others) until his business grew bigger. He now shipped six-figure sums' worth of DVDs and other electronic goods, making a profit of US$18,000 on each shipment. CJ was one of the lucky ones – or the astute ones, depending on your point of view. He had succeeded where some African traders had failed, establishing a life in China where others had fallen victim to swindlers back home. These fraudsters had turned some ambitious short-term immigrants into visa-overstayers, drug dealers, prostitutes, men and women who wandered the streets aimlessly, corralled into a life of peccadillos or heavy crime, and judged on face value by much of China.

'What kind of reasons do people back home give you for not handing over the money?' I asked CJ.

'They might tell you all sorts of stories . . . They sent it to a customer and the customer never paid . . . different stories. Sometimes they tell you that the stuff cannot sell. The stock is in the warehouse.'

'But then they'd have to show you the stock if they say it's not selling?'

'But they are not there. Most of the guys here don't have papers or passports. They cannot return home. They wash plates to survive, or cook for this lady.' CJ pointed at the restaurant proprietor standing in the corner, a friendly Filipina woman who was married to a Nigerian.

'Have you ever met someone who's stolen your money here back in Nigeria?'

'Yes,' CJ nodded.

'So how do you deal with that? What was your reaction?'

'You can't do anything anyway. You just call the police. That person will then bribe the police. So the police will tell you, "Sorry, this guy doesn't have the money." Let's assume he owes you one million naira. The police will then say, "OK, this guy is going to pay you twenty thousand a month until he's finished the debt." And then they will be talking to you like you have no choice. You don't know what to do. You leave it to God.'

'Did the guy ever pay you back?'

CJ shook his head. 'He can't. Most people in my position, they will find thugs to deal with it. That's if you have the mind, you know?'

'What do these thugs do?'

'They beat him up, threaten him. Some of the thieves are afraid. Some don't care.'

CJ confirmed the stories I'd heard in Guangzhou about traders in China being betrayed by friends and relatives back in Africa. CJ said that a man once entrusted his goods and hard-earned profits to his parents in Nigeria, only for the elders to donate it – in good conscience, of course – to their charismatic (and wealthy) church pastor. The man was so livid he reported his parents to the police and had them arrested.

I cast my mind back to the day Egisimba threw himself

out of the Tangqi building. I had struggled to comprehend how fear of deportation could compel a man to choose near-certain death and leap fifty-five feet out of a window. Nigeria can be a very tough place to live, true, but it is perfectly habitable. Fear of Chinese prisons may have played a role. Another part of the answer lay in the relationship between Africans (Nigerians, specifically) and their people back home on the continent. There was a complexity I hadn't fully understood.

Ikem, the jeweller in Sanyuanli, had explained that returning to Nigeria could be a death sentence in itself. He described a scenario similar to that outlined by CJ. A man like Egisimba may have been cheated by a friend back home, someone who stole the profits from merchandise Egisimba had sent there. With no effective recourse to Nigerian law enforcement, Egisimba might have arranged for thugs to beat up the person who cheated him. This swindler, on hearing about Egisimba's imminent return, tries to beat him up or even kill him as a pre-emptive measure. And so in that moment when Emmanuel Egisimba paused on the window-sill of the Tangqi building, he may have believed he was caught between a rock and a hard place.

'It must be so stressful when you're here and someone has stolen your money back home,' I said to CJ.

'They don't have heart, you know? Those guys are bullshitters. Their heart is cold. In Hong Kong we don't have good job opportunities. And then if you want to work here you must have document. I have a document to work here. I could get a job like security job . . . like bouncer in a club, or work for a construction company. That's what most guys do because they can't do Nigerian business.

'Those who can eat my money are few. They know I'll always come back, and I have people in the market there. But if you are living here and you send it back home you might be sorry. That is why when you are in Guangzhou you'll see a lot of guys walking around looking for money just to eat food. Sometimes they sell their passports to survive. So that's how it is. It's crazy. Very, very crazy.'

'Do the Chinese make it hard for Nigerians?'

'Chinese guys, they are very good people,' CJ said. 'You know like when you do business with them, they trust people like Nigerians. You know, Nigerians trust people too much in terms of business. Someone could just come to your shop and buy your goods one or two times, then the next time talk about getting credit. And you just do it. That is how the Chinese do. But sometimes our people fuck up with them because they will give you these goods and you send it back home, the people will not record the money. You'll lose that connection and then you'll end up in the street. You'll be stranded. Most of the guys, they don't have a house to live in, you know?'

'I didn't know it was that bad,' I said. 'They don't tell you much.'

'They can't tell you much 'cause it's not easy. I'll send a container now and it's already in Nigeria. I don't go because my staff is there. I have six workers. They're all girls, no boys. My sister is my manager.'

'Why just girls?'

'Because once you get these guys they will like to be the boss. And they want to build their own house. They want to marry, you know? But these girls, they only need money to buy make-up, clothes and food, so it's OK. Every month you pay them and they'll be happy. Sometimes you just dash them some money.' I bit my tongue at the sexism and continued nodding. 'I'll go to China by next week and load another container.'

I spent the rest of the evening with CJ and a bunch of his Nigerian friends. They were a mix of traders and former professional footballers. Some of them lived in Hong Kong, others in China and Australia. They were all middle-aged men with proper documentation to live in their respective countries. Content and relaxed, CJ & co. were living their best lives and enjoying the kind of mobility people in the developed world take for granted.

—

As a single guy, CJ's life seemed tidy and uncomplicated. By now I was used to hearing stories about families being split across continents as a result of China's unsympathetic visa regime. The situation forced some people into highly unorthodox arrangements, so I discovered.

I was back in Chungking Mansions where, in the middle of the ground-floor corridor, two Indian men stood, arms folded, legs planted wide apart, forcing everyone to squeeze past them. It was all very strange and aggressive and juvenile.

In the elevator on my way to my hotel room, I got chatting to a tall, lanky, silver-bearded Nigerian man who looked well into his fifties. I warmed to him immediately. His name was Samson, and he was manager of a guesthouse on one of the upper floors. He invited me to take a look. In an unoccupied room, we each sat on one of the twin beds and chatted like brother and sister.

Samson used to export textiles from Hong Kong. But then the factories moved to China, and now the Chinese were selling the fabrics in Nigeria itself, squeezing out local businesses. Samson consequently decided to live in Hong Kong permanently and manage this hotel.

I immediately complained to him about the Asian guys blocking everyone's path in the corridor on the ground floor of Chungking Mansions.

'That is their problem. You see, those Pakistanis are very arrogant. Every time, they love fighting too much.'

'Are they looking for a fight when they stand like that?'

He chuckled. 'You just mind yourself. Actually, they will not fight you. The only thing is that most of them they smoke weed, take cocaine. After they have smoked they will go and misbehave.'

'Who do they fight?' I asked.

'Maybe some people buy drugs from them, no pay them money. Some groups can come from another place to come and beat the person. Or maybe they fight for ladies . . . or they go to club and fight. They like problem too much. The Hong Kong police will put them in cells for two days, three days. Four days later you see them outside again.' Samson smiled. 'If you don't see them on the ground floor for one month, two month, the next month you will see them again!

'They know they cannot confront Africans, one or two people. If they want to confront Africans they will reinforce themselves. All these Igbo boys already show them pepper. Two or three policemen?' Samson made a swiping sound. 'Fighters scattered them! After that the police reinforce. They no have power. They know these people are very strong, o.'

The brazenness of those troublemakers was shocking.

'But Hong Kong is very peaceful,' he said. 'If you mind your own business and you have small business, it's OK for you.'

Every December Samson returned to Nigeria to visit his family.

'I have four children in Nigeria. And I marry here,' he told me.

'Did you have to divorce your wife in Nigeria?'

'No, my wife is still in Nigeria. And I have another wife here.'

'Does your Nigerian wife know?'

Samson shrugged. 'She knows I have kids here, no problem.'

'But are you allowed to have two wives?'

'Let me tell you: if you want to do things, you need to use your mind. You need to use your wisdom. You understand what I mean? Most of the people who marry here already have family in Nigeria. My tribe, the Yoruba, from age twenty, twenty-five they worry you: "Go marry, go marry". If you enter thirty and you have not marry . . . wow, your family will conduct meeting! "Why you are not married? Tell us, what is your problem".' Samson laughed. 'So I already know the Hong Kong system before I stay. You present a certificate from Nigeria to say you have a divorce. Finish. But my wife here know everything.' He clapped his hands. 'If you love somebody you ask her. If you want, do. If you don't want, don't do.'

'Does your Hong Kong wife love you?' I asked.

Samson frowned at me quizzically. 'Why? Why not love?'

'So it's a marriage for love?'

'Yeaaaah!' he roared with a smile.

'But does your wife in Nigeria know that you married for love?'

'Why would she not know? Let me tell you about my tribes. I come from a bona fide Christian family, you understand? We cannot marry two wives. But my wife's family are all Muslims. So in their family they have maaaany wives. Her father has forty wives.'

I was incredulous. 'Do you mean four zero or fourteen?'

'Four zero! My wife is the last-born of her father. She is number ninety-nine, I'm telling you! So when I tell my wife the situation like this in Hong Kong and we need to take care of the children . . . she needs to comply. There's no problem.'

'So your kids know?'

'Why will they not know? There is no problem.'

Samson's children had never visited Hong Kong but he wanted his youngest, an eleven-year-old boy, to come and live here. 'Even my Chinese wife here say I should bring my son. My wife and I we have tried but she is not pregnant. She don't have any baby. Everything is in the hand of God. So her mother also said we should bring my son so my wife can take care of him because she no have.'

'But her mother will have a grandson who is Nigerian,' I remarked. 'She doesn't mind?'

Samson laughed and clapped his hands. 'Noooo. There's no problem. Let me tell you: life is very simple, if you can understand life. In Nigeria my children do not lack anything. They do not have problem. They live peacefully. You try your best for the family. If they do not lack anything it's OK. Only if they are not eating can they complain that you have another wife. Do you understand what I mean?'

'Don't the Chinese dislike Black people?' I asked Samson.

'Nooooo! That is before, o! *Now*? No. Even my wife tell me one of her friends is looking for Black men. Because the Chinese men . . . when their wife get to thirty or thirty-two, they look for another woman. That is why they don't like their men. So when they are getting to age thirty, thirty-one, thirty-two, thirty-three, the men go to China and take young ladies. All Hong Kong men go to China. Because China have many ladies.'

'As girlfriends, prostitutes or wives?'

'Prostitute. *Many* in China. You know China is very big. You have *maaany* girls. The Hong Kong boys, they go to Shenzhen – just HK$50 transport – and come back. I'm telling you!'

He was right. In southern China in the 1980s and 1990s, wealthy Hong Kong men often had a 'second wife', i.e. mistresses in the form of young migrant women from rural areas.

'So that is why Hong Kong ladies love Blacks. Maybe before long time they don't. But now civilisation has already opened many eyes. Things have already changed.'

Samson was incredibly relaxed about his family arrangements. Where I saw complexity he saw a means to an end. He surfed any tumult with the calmness of a patriarch in control, relying on his Chinese wife's open-minded flexibility and his Nigerian wife's traditional acceptance.

The Chinese often accused Africans of polygamy, or marrying for money and other unromantic benefits. Samson's story would undoubtedly appal them. But, put in the same situation, Chinese immigrants in Africa behave no differently. In his book *China's Second Continent*, American journalist Howard French met Chinese men in southern Africa who admitted to marrying local women as a way of obtaining residency so that they could purchase land and businesses. One man from Hubei Province justified his actions by quoting the Chinese expression: 'You leap forward if there's an empty space.' He told his wife back home that marrying a Namibian woman was the only way to extend his visa in that country.

We like to think of money as generally profane or vulgar, while marriage is sacred. But in reality, anything that helps us survive becomes sacred. The entanglement of money and marriage, so unseemly in our modern romantic times, becomes inevitable when survival is at stake.

—

Migration, in many ways, is more a man's game. Guys like Samson can devise unorthodox family structures, weave all manner of polyamorous, cross-racial, quasi-adoption tangles, and scatter their seed to the wind when there's nearly always a female to suck up the consequences and provide stability. For female African migrants, however, the situation could be very different, as I soon found out.

Across the street from Chungking was the 7-Eleven convenience store, where all sections of Hong Kong society fleetingly rubbed shoulders. It was an improbable mix of middle-aged middle Englanders on holiday, African visa overstayers, Chinese mainlanders and Hong Kong old-timers, all buying snacks and drinks.

One evening, while buying a pack of my beloved Ferrero Rocher, a chubby woman stopped me at the entrance steps.

'Hello! You – I saw you this morning in Chungking!' she told me in a booming voice. 'Where are you from?'

Ayanda was her name. Bulging South African eyes and a wide, bulbous nose. Her hair weave, streaked with red, was covered with a purple baseball cap. Standing beside her was her eighteen-month-old daughter, a bundle of cuteness called Bongi who was determined to run to the nearby metro entrance. I held out my arm to stop her.

'Just let her go,' Ayanda said with an air of resignation. She meant it. Bongi left the 7-Eleven and toddled along the pavement towards the station. I couldn't bear to see the child running off alone like that, so I followed her and restrained her at the top of the stairs. She wriggled and screamed. Heads were turning. Me, the abductor. I released Bongi and let her clod-hop down the stairs and sprint into a crowd of evening commuters. This was getting ridiculous. Wasn't her mother concerned? She had known me all of two minutes yet had trusted her baby with me. Towards the ticket barriers I scooped Bongi up in my arms and returned her, wriggling and screaming, to the 7-Eleven.

Ayanda was now in the back corner of the shop, knocking back a mini bottle of cabernet sauvignon. She offered me a sip while telling me about Bongi's birth. Her daughter was born premature in 2014. Since her father, a Nigerian, was a refugee in Hong Kong, Bongi was given free medi-cation and incubation for seven weeks; the UN footed the bill.

'The baby in the birth certificate is under his name. But he's a piece of shit,' Ayanda said. 'He doesn't want to take care of the baby. He just fucks around and everything, so I dumped him . . . Me, I just take the baby, I take my clothes and the baby's boots . . . I left him. But you know, any time he wants he can just take her.'

'Really?'

'Because the baby is under his name. But so far so good because I'm good with the baby. She's clean, right?'

I nodded.

'Is she smelling bad?'

I shook my head.

'She's got everything . . . food, diapers, everything.' Ayanda sounded defensive, as if she was used to accusations of neglect.

'Does her father want to see her?' I asked.

'He wants to see her but he doesn't want to call me. We don't talk. Bongi will talk to him but he and his friends, they like to smoke weed. That's the truth.'

'What's Bongi's nationality?'

'She's half South African, half Nigerian and born in Hong Kong,' Ayanda smiled proudly. 'I want the baby to have a Nigerian passport but because the father is a refugee he cannot sign. He's an overstayer in Hong Kong.'

Bongi ran off down an aisle. Ayanda shouted after her in a very loud voice: 'Come back here!' Everyone in the shop turned to look at this screaming woman. Alcohol had stripped away all her inhibitions. I was getting a little embarrassed. That corner of the 7-Eleven was popular among Africans because it offered free wifi, and therefore became a spot for socialising.

Ayanda had come from South Africa three years previously and worked in the entertainment industry. Now that she had Hong Kong residency, she wanted to put Bongi under a South African passport. Ideally Bongi would have all passports and a Hong Kong residency ID. 'Then when she grows up and she wants to go to school and study, she's powerful already. She will make a choice. She's a star!' Ayanda grinned and kissed Bongi and stared into the girl's eyes. 'Ay, mama . . . you are so beautiful.' Ayanda turned to me. 'When she grows up she will be speaking all the languages! Sometimes she even speaks Arabic because our friends here they are speaking Arabic.'

Ayanda pointed towards the three North African men who had just entered the shop. They cuddled Bongi and chatted with her. The girl had surrogate uncles and aunts from all over the world.

Bongi grinned a very cute grin. It made everyone smile. 'The smile is priceless!' Ayanda gushed. 'Even if she makes you angry, when she starts smiling you are like, Lord let me do anything she says. She looks like her father. He is sooo handsome. If you see him you will want to bang him.'

Ayanda cuddled Bongi again. 'You Nigerian woman, you!' Then she turned to me again: 'Noo, everybody says, "This baby is too beautiful for you." I believe them because, you know, I am not beautiful. She looks like her father.'

There was no denying it – Bongi looked nothing like Ayanda.

'She's got your spirit,' I replied.

'I know the baby don't look like me. You too . . . be honest. She don't look like me, right? So that means I'm ugly.'

'No, it doesn't mean you're ugly. It just means she has her father's face.'

'Everybody says, "Ah, you are too ugly for this baby".'

Bongi did have a cute face. Her vaguely epicanthic eyes narrowed at the corners. She had a little upturned nose and an adorable smile – her top lip was unusually thin; the philtrum was smooth to the point of non-existence and lent an unusual curviness to her grin. Then it hit me: Bongi had foetal alcohol syndrome. The signs were written all over her features.

We walked back to Chungking Mansions across the street. A shabby corridor at the back of the building on the ground floor was where Nigerians congregated every evening. Music, chairs, tables, and shops lined the corridor. From behind a bar a man sold alcohol to a crowd that was, as usual, predominantly male.

Ayanda was now wielding a large bottle of red. 'I like it mellow,' she said, with the voice of a connoisseur. She and Bongi lived in one of the rooms upstairs, a room with a double bed. She pointed to one of the men sitting at a table behind us. 'That is Bongi's daddy.' The man looked like her, albeit without the foetal alcohol syndrome features, like a healthier prototype of his daughter. He and half the men around him were drug dealers, Ayanda claimed. And he didn't contribute financially to her upbringing. He beat Ayanda too, allegedly.

Bongi was hanging around her father, staring up at his face. He did not acknowledge Ayanda or me. He didn't talk with Bongi much, either; the reggae was pounding too loudly.

'Did you see him touching her?' Ayanda remarked. 'I like it when he touches her. Even though he's a piece of shit I still love him. I hope we can be together again one day.'

She told me her babyfather's drug dealer friends persuaded him to sleep around after she got pregnant. When she caught him with another woman, 'I gave him a black eye. In public.'

There was no way of verifying Ayanda's version of events but it was clear she and her baby's father were not on speaking terms. No eye contact, nothing. Ayanda claimed he slept around with Indonesian and Filipina women. The Filipinas she was particularly disdainful of, collectively dismissing them as 'whores'.

By now it was 10.30 p.m. and Bongi was still awake. Ayanda didn't enforce a sleeping routine. The child toddled round the corner out of sight for a good two minutes. When I rose from my chair to look for her, Ayanda told me to relax: 'She always comes back to me. Look –' Ayanda pointed to an effeminate Indian guy who was now cradling Bongi '– everybody loves her.'

The Nigerian men took turns to pinch her cheeks or give her high-fives and fist bumps when she waddled past them. At one point the child imitated her male elders by wedging a toothpick between her lips. Ayanda found this hilarious. One of the older men (sitting on the 'good', non-drug-dealer table) didn't. He snatched the toothpick out of Bongi's mouth and gave Ayanda a judgemental glare.

A Vietnamese-looking woman walked past our table and down the corridor. Her eyes smiled vacantly, and beneath her shabby fur-lined coat was a sweater stretched over her significantly pregnant belly. No trousers or skirt, just bare legs and a hint of crotch. Clearly she had mental health problems. The woman's face lit up when she saw Bongi. As she interacted with the toddler, Ayanda approached her and pulled down her sweater for her to protect her modesty.

'She may not even know who the father is,' Ayanda remarked as she returned to her seat. 'She'll sleep with anyone because she's mental.'

There weren't many other places to stay in Hong Kong if you were a non-Chinese immigrant or asylum seeker or unskilled jobseeker. A small, densely populated island with some of the highest property prices in the world. In Chungking you had to live with your mistakes. Couples like Ayanda and her babyfather could be separated emotionally, but were physically bound by this place. There was nowhere to escape. You shit where you sleep.

—

In the Central district of Hong Kong, a stone's throw from GAP, Marks & Spencer and other British and American shops, I sat down in a café frequented by British corporate workers. Heeled and suited, they sipped coffee and murmured in low, southern English voices. I was there to meet Vuyi Colossa, an athlete who, like CJ, had also carved out a successful life in the city.

He and I had no problem spotting one another as we were the only two Black people in the joint. He shook my hand and muscles flexed beneath his dark blue polo shirt. When I remarked that he looked bigger than a lightweight, a dimpled smile spread across his face.

'I stopped fighting three years ago,' he replied, and I cringed on realising I had basically told him he was out of shape.

I first came across Vuyi in the *China Daily* newspaper. Born in South Africa, he is a former mixed-martial-arts champion who dispatched his opponents with an extremely fast jab that earned him the fighting name 'Cheetah'. He now lived in Hong Kong and was enjoying a successful life here with his Chinese wife and their two children, which was a refreshing change from his compatriot, Ayanda. Unlike many Africans in Guangzhou, Vuyi was forthcoming about his backstory, which revealed a personality conducive to carving out a life in the Far East. He was loud and enthusiastic, his thoughts erupting in bursts. At times he spoke so quickly his words tripped over themselves, and I struggled to keep up.

The eldest of five, Vuyi was born in the Free State in 1982 in a township called Brandfort, where Winnie Mandela was exiled. It was a middle-class neighbourhood, the type with brick houses and gates and front gardens. All was well until his father lost his job, and suddenly Vuyi had to move in with relatives at the poor end of the township – no toilets, no water, just tin shacks with walls so flimsy you couldn't even bang them in frustration.

It was 1994, the dying days of apartheid, and Vuyi heard that the mainly white, fee-paying boys' school had started admitting Black pupils. He applied without his mother's knowledge, was accepted and even secured a fee waiver after a teacher probed him about his financial circumstances. The school was in the same middle-class area where Vuyi had previously lived. Passing his former bourgeois home after classes was an indignity he had to stomach each day.

His white school's curriculum offered the 'white' sport of kickboxing, rather than boxing, which is favoured by Blacks. 'I thought, "Let me do kickboxing . . . I'm going to be the first one!"' Vuyi's eyes lit up. 'In the whole class I was the only Black guy.' He was also small for his age. After his first session Vuyi didn't return home because he lived twenty kilometres away and it was impossible to get taxis at night.

'I packed my bag as if I was going back, but I stayed.'
Sometimes he did do the twenty-kilometre walk back home,
fuelled by a diet of pap, maize meal, peaches from the neighbourhood tree and spinach from the garden. There was meat,
but only in the first three weeks of the month.

'When I see these people eating expensive organic vegetables and quinoa, I laugh,' Vuyi said. His sporting success
earned him prefect status, and he was disciplining the white
boys despite his diminutive stature. 'I wasn't scared of them.
I would deal with them very quickly.' During school breaks
the boys would get their gloves and punch each other. One
morning, huge white boys lined up to test their skills against
Vuyi. He dispatched them one by one. 'From that day the
whole school said, "This motherfucker is dangerous!"' Vuyi
laughed as he made slapping motions with his hands.

One day his kickboxing trainer, a burly Afrikaner
policeman called Wouter, decided to take Vuyi under his
wing.

'Wouter made this mission for me to succeed. He sent
tapes to me, training methods and stuff. And from there I
competed in lots of competitions, getting this title, that title,
you know?' Tears welled up in Vuyi's eyes. 'He passed away
a few years ago.'

Excelling at national level came easily to Vuyi. But lily-
white South African kickboxing found it hard to accept a
Black kid as champion. Vuyi claims he was regularly declared
the loser in bouts even though he had clearly won them. 'I
kicked his ass, everybody sees – but he still wins. To win I
had to beat somebody really bad. That was a lesson for me.
And today it still happens. I went to Korea and fight – they
rob you. But I kept on. Back then I didn't understand. I

didn't care. I was just focusing on the sport, I didn't focus on the politics of it. I remember when I got into the South African trials they didn't announce it in the stadium. They only told me afterwards,' he chuckled. Yet two weeks later Vuyi was pronounced sportsman of the year, and 'from then, that's when they saw me different'.

After graduating high school he moved to Pretoria and went on to become the South African kickboxing champion in 2003, and was runner-up in the WAKO Professional World Championship. Then he was invited to fight in Japan, his first visit to Asia. It was en route back to South Africa that he first visited Hong Kong, on a passing visit. 'I saw big buildings; the streets – it was a Sunday – were full of helpers [domestic staff]. Beautiful *female* helpers. That time I was twenty-five, testosterone was super high. *Look at that, oh my god, amazing!* I was going crazy.'

Vuyi returned to Korea later that year for another fight and went on to win even more. When a promoter then asked him to move to Hong Kong in 2008, he packed his bags gleefully. He won major bouts in Hong Kong and in mainland China before moving into mixed martial arts (MMA). There were reality TV show appearances. Then he began promoting MMA matches, including the world's first tournament for white-collar workers, held in Hong Kong. Now he promotes professional fights for men and women in Hong Kong. He also runs a foundation to build a bridge between Africa and Asia in martial arts. 'I want to make it easier for the other kids coming after me.'

Vuyi busies himself promoting events, attending black-tie soirees for fundraising. He was in talks with a Macao investor who wanted to put HK$1 billion in a joint venture.

'In Hong Kong itself, you've just got to know your bearings. All my life I have lived for myself, to do what I want, not to please other people. I guess that's why I was able to survive . . . there's crazy money here. I never imagined I would be talking to billionaires . . . never.'

How did being a minority in school in South Africa compare with being a minority in Hong Kong? I asked.

'Where I've been is tough, so for me this is easy. To do business you have to be ten times better than everyone else. Number one: you're not from here. Two: you are last on the list.' By 'list' Vuyi meant the ethno-social hierarchy that puts white men at the top, followed by Chinese, then other Asians, then Africans at the bottom. 'Only *you* understand your dream. To make someone else understand your dream and believe in it is hard.'

Vuyi's dream was made possible by a Hong Kong Chinese woman who worked in insurance and investment sales and went on to become his wife and mother of his two children. They met through mutual friends in Hong Kong. Does having a Chinese wife help in his business dealings with the Chinese?

'The Hong Kong way of doing things is like the West. The mainlanders' way of doing things is more like South Africa. But in a way it helps to have a Chinese wife because sometimes I'll come to a place before my wife comes. The Chinese treat me like shit, then she'll come and I'll pretend like I don't know her. They see her respecting me, then they change their tune.'

The racism, Vuyi pointed out, is 'equal opportunity'. 'I'm not the only one,' he laughed. 'When a Chinese person says, "screw the foreigner" you know they mean *everybody*!'

In Mandarin there are derogatory names for everyone and anyone, including within Chinese society: *dong yi* means 'east barbarian'; *nan man* is 'south barbarian'; '*xi rong*' is west barbarian, and *bei di* means 'north barbarian'. Foreigners are called *gui* ('devils'), or *hei gui* ('black devils') or *Kunlun nu* ('Kunlun slaves'). Whites are *yang guizi* ('foreign devils'), *hong mao gui* ('red-haired devils'), *fangou* ('barbarian dog'). Then there's *gui lao* ('male devil') and *gui po* ('female devil').

Vuyi's wife helped him read the Chinese-language documents for background checks on potential investment partners. She accompanied him on trips to China and translated for him. Picking up Mandarin was quite easy, Vuyi said, but he has been slow to learn Cantonese.

'How did your wife's parents react when they first met you?' I asked him.

He smiled: 'Everything I do is strategy . . . I always think about strategy. The first time I met the in-laws my wife brought her mother only. Because I know if I meet the mother first she can soften up the dad. Meet the mother first. Charm the mum. We learnt this stuff in South Africa when you're growing up and dating girls. My wife didn't tell her mother that I'm Black. She knew that I was a foreigner, but not Black. There are layers: there's white,' he sliced downwards into the air repeatedly, 'pah, pah, pah, pah . . . then Black. We're always at the bottom of the list. I met her mum in public on purpose so that she couldn't freak out that much. She came and sat down, asked me questions. Then I went to meet the dad. He said, "I don't like you." Why? Because I'm Black? I thought, you know what? It's OK – I'm from South Africa. I've been discriminated against all of my life . . . kids calling me names, whatever. So I told her dad,

"Anything you want to do has to top *that*." If he doesn't top it then he might as well forget it. He's talking to the wrong person.'

Vuyi asked his wife to explain this to her father, but she didn't need to: she became pregnant, so her father changed his attitude.

'When my son was born, we were in the hospital. My wife asked for her glasses to see the baby. First thing she said was, "Oh my god, he's so white!" I'm thinking, What do you expect? She has a baby with a Black guy and the baby comes out black? Nooooo! My son was Chinese-looking but they could tell he was a mix.'

It seems the way to mollify Chinese in-laws is to give them grandchildren and to be financially successful.

'Do you have close Chinese friends?' I asked Vuyi.

'Close, close friends? I don't have. My close friends are my family. Last time I saw my high school friends was in high school. We grew apart.' Many of his shanty town friends were dead, he told me. Even his high school girlfriend. He had recently returned to South Africa to attend her funeral.

'Do you feel isolated in Hong Kong?' I asked.

'What's isolation? It's good to be unique. It's not a curse. You think it's a curse in the beginning when people are teasing you. But then you make it. It's great. I won't make noise in Hong Kong,' Vuyi said. 'I don't like to make a grand entry. Spending time with myself, the kids and the family . . . that I love. I entertain people once in a while. This is a great place.'

It didn't surprise me that Vuyi was a bit of a loner. Very few people shared his breadth of life experience, culturally and socio-economically. The ability to seek out a life in a place as alien as Hong Kong took a certain kind of maverick, outlier mentality.

'Hong Kong for me has been good. If there is something you want to do, it allows it. You can have money or not have money . . . it's all about how you play the game. I have always been independent. I had to take care of my siblings. I believe in doing things for yourself and then you look for help.'

Vuyi took one last sip of his coffee.

'I was telling my wife about the process of bamboo and how it grows. You know how it grows? If you plant it here, it will grow twenty metres away. The root spreads out first, so you won't know its origin. By the time it comes out you try to find the original place where it was planted, but you can't find it. It's strong and you don't know how to take it out. I like to think of myself like that mentally. Whatever plans I'm doing will be like bamboo.'

—

After my coffee with Vuyi, I walked across town to a visa agency. I was applying for my third entry visa into mainland China. On each of my previous applications at this particular agency they had revised the price upward, the receptionist scribbling the new amount on a sheet of paper. Not once was I shown an official, typed-up price guide. I later discovered that white people with the same British passport as me were charged lower amounts. Nevertheless, my applications had all been successful.

Not this time.

The woman behind the counter slapped my passport down and said harshly, 'No visa! No visa for you!'

'Why?'

'You born in Nigeria. New rules. They don't want anybody born in Nigeria.'

'But I've never even lived there! I'm a UK citizen!'

The lady shrugged her shoulders.

I was incredulous. My British passport was supposed to be my protection, the buffer against prejudice, my ticket to the world. But Guangdong law says that if an alien's visa application is denied, the visa-issuing unit is not obliged to give a reason. The reality of life as an African under China's arbitrary visa policy was brought home to me fully that day. I left the office shaken and despondent. For me the stakes had felt high – I had a book to research and write. But I felt a deep empathy for those whose lives and livelihoods depended on re-entering China; people for whom so much was at stake, including marriages and access to half-Chinese children. The uncertainty must be unbearable. For help, I called upon my contacts – Chinese expats with just a few degrees of separation from government. I was fortunate to be able to have such recourse, unlike most Africans here. But it didn't help, ultimately. Days later, I tried a different visa agency and thankfully managed to get my visa this time. The stress and unpredictability did nothing for my health, though. I celebrated by having a duck rice dish at a restaurant nearby.

—

On my final morning in Hong Kong I decided to get a leg wax before returning to the mainland. A mainland treatment would've been cheaper but I was scared of doing it with the language barrier.

The aesthetician was on the upper floors of a building in Tsim Sha Tsui, one block away from Chungking Mansions.

'Are you allergic to any penicillin?' asked the lady behind the reception desk.

'No,' I replied, feeling slightly confused. I was just here for hair removal.

We were sitting in an office in surroundings that were pristinely white and surgical.

'Have you had any surgery recently?' the lady continued. I couldn't tell if she was a doctor or just a manager. She had already made me fill out a form requesting my full medical history.

I was sent to an adjacent, low-lit room where another woman, dressed in white, smiled at me behind a surgical mask. She laid me down on a high bed, then angled a bright light over my body. I was beginning to get nervous . . . were they harvesting my organs? I only wanted a wax! But I was too British to speak up and ask impertinent questions, so I closed my eyes and prepared for life without a kidney.

Mercifully, the procedure turned out to be a strip wax after all. I returned to Chungking Mansions, packed my bags and took a train back to the mainland.

IX

HE WHO WALKS ALONE

I arrived at Guangzhou's massive modern train station. As my taxi cruised along the elevated road that curved towards the arrivals area, several parked bullet trains came into view. They were a glory to behold: long and gleaming white with rounded black noses, like Boeing snakes. The station, Asia's largest, looks like an airport – which is fitting considering that domestic travel bears all the hallmarks of an international flight, complete with mandatory passport and baggage security checks.

I was heading to the city of Wuhan in Hubei Province to meet an academic by the name of Professor Zhigang Li, who had overseen research on Africans in China and – praise be – spoke English.

Before boarding my train, I paused on the platform to gawp at the majesty of my surroundings. Palm trees swayed by the open-sided platforms, and sunshine poured through the glass, latticed, banana-leaf-style roof.

I boarded a first-class carriage on a train bound for Wuhan. Rarely do I travel first class on any mode of transport, so the arriviste in me was deliriously impressed. The compartment contained just four chairs – wide, comfy, red velvet recliners with legroom for giants, power sockets and large windows. I took selfies and grinned smugly. I was behaving exactly like those domestic tourists whom I privately mocked for taking selfies in front of security signs and other banal bits of aviation architecture. We were all the same, submitting to the shock and awe of ultra-modern transport.

I made myself comfortable. The train moved through Guangdong and Hunan provinces. Quarries and reservoirs were followed by farmland, orange groves, rice paddies and the occasional massive river. We zoomed past fish farms, and little farmhouses standing among patches of yellow rapeseed. A few bamboo groves made brief appearances, as did a cluster of graves on a hillside. The sunlight beaming into the eastern windows was low and resplendent, an orangey glow against mountains that were arranged in folds of different shades of green.

The train travelled so fast that we experienced various microclimates. One minute it was all golden sunshine, then we emerged from a tunnel into a thick grey fog; clouds of mist nestled between those mountain folds. A minute later it was summertime again.

At the Wuhan terminal, after most passengers had disembarked, I lingered on the train and watched as an employee swivelled the rows of seats in the second-class carriages so that they faced the opposite direction for the return journey. With a bend of her hips, the lady grabbed one row of seats with her right arm and swung it violently so that it swivelled one hundred and eighty degrees. She then used her left arm to do the same with the seats on the other side before moving on to the next row and repeating the action. The job needed completing throughout the train before the next batch of passengers boarded. She swung row after row, through carriage after carriage, with mesmeric vigour. Her work seemed a very humane consideration towards sufferers of motion sickness, but at what cost to her spine, I wondered.

Outside the station I queued for a taxi at the biggest taxi rank I've ever laid eyes on. Perhaps seventy cars arranged as if in a car park. I have never seen so many taxis in one place. Everything about Wuhan was vast. The bridge my taxi cruised along was an impressive 1,876 metres long and twenty-six metres wide, its bridgeheads soaring ninety metres above us. It traversed the mighty Yangtze River, the world's third longest waterway, whose drainage basin occupies a fifth of China's land surface. I couldn't help being impressed by this infrastructure, yet fearful of its consequences, what with China being the world's biggest emitter of carbon. Energy consumption, energy production, air pollution – the optimism of high growth now replaced by a fear of its consequences. China's 'dormant' years under Chairman Mao had bought humankind a few more years in our acceleration towards an environmental reckoning, while Africa's slow economic growth had also bought the planet some extra time.

As my taxi crossed the Yangtze River, it was hard to imagine it as anything other than a watery interlude in the urban sprawl, but the river is still home to some alligators, sturgeons, narrow-ridged finless porpoises and river dolphins, though they are now endangered. And there were species, such as the Chinese paddlefish, that I didn't know existed but discovered only when reading about their extinction. Intrigue and disappointment all in one go: known as the 'Chinese swordfish', it had a long snout and grew to almost ten feet long. It lived in the sea but swam upriver to spawn, an annual migration pattern that was later disrupted by the building of the gigantic hydro-electric Three Gorges Dam. Their populations became fragmented and isolated. Then humans added to the annihilation through overfishing. The last live specimen was seen in 2003. Now a preserved specimen lies suspended in all its shiny and curvaceous beauty in a glass tank in Wuhan's Museum of Hydrobiological Sciences at the Institute of Hydrobiology.

Once my taxi reached the other bank of the river, we entered the enormity of Wuhan city, where the highways were three lanes wide each way. Big, blocky skyscrapers and a forest of cranes loomed in the smoggy distance.

Little did I know then that I was at the epicentre of an event that would affect the entire world. On New Year's Eve 2019, epidemiologists at the Chinese Center for Disease Control and Prevention reported several cases of pneumonia in this city. Less than a fortnight later, the World Health Organization (WHO) announced that a new coronavirus, SARS-CoV-2, had been identified, and by March 2020 a global pandemic was declared. Although the source of the original outbreak remains undetermined, Wuhan would be the first major city in the world to go into full lockdown.

It's almost fitting that the world's greatest pandemic in over a century emerged from this behemoth of a conurbation. The COVID-19 virus is a reflection of our modern world, its transmission made possible by technology, high population densities and high mobility. The very mobility that brought me to Wuhan would later confine me to a flat in north London for much of 2020 and 2021. But for now, I was a carefree traveller.

I arrived at my hotel and queued at the reception behind

a long-haired woman who wore an oversized white sports jacket, white baseball cap, white-rimmed sunglasses and white high-wedge trainers, and was making demands in an officious tone. I dumped my bags in my room and immediately headed to the subway station on Jinjiang Road. By now I was able to ask for directions in Chinese. The station was staffed by people in a garishly camp combination of purple coats and red sashes. Wuhan is so massive that each station is widely spaced apart. My destination, Guangbutun, though only about eight stops away, took an age to reach.

At a café there, I met Professor Li, Dean of the School of Urban Design at Wuhan University. He was genial and stocky, the same height as me and the exact same age. I was ecstatic to finally be interacting with a Chinese person who not only spoke good English but had an interest in the Africans living here. Their story as migrants, he said, parallels that of China's 200 million rural-to-urban migrants who face similar restrictions and some discrimination.

'Except the government is giving Chinese rural migrants more freedom,' Zhigang said. 'You need people to consume, to buy houses and stay in the city. So the central government is pushing the local governments to loosen their control over rural migrants. It's different with Africans.'

I agreed. There was an exceptionalism around sub-Saharans. Anti-immigration online commentators often expressed concerns about 'purity of culture' but such reasoning was disingenuous. The Chinese sip Brazilian coffee and French champagne, and they wear Nike everything. What cultural threat did Africans pose? Chinese people are hardly in danger of speaking Igbo instead of Mandarin, or dropping their egg fried rice in favour of jollof.

'What's the strangest thing you've learned about China?' Zhigang asked me. I told him I couldn't get over its contradictions: so strict yet so liberal; conservative yet tolerant. He nodded. 'The image of China is very complicated. Everything is OK until you get to politics. The red line is the politics.'

I mentioned how many of the people seemed untroubled by the lack of democracy.

'As long as you can make money,' Zhigang replied. He gave an example of a recent demonstration in northern China. 'The mining plant went bankrupt and they didn't pay two thousand workers. So the workers went out onto the street to demonstrate. That's a real problem. If you are disadvantaged then you have to take political action. If you're on the side of advantage, then you don't need to be very political.' This was true of most societies around the world.

'How did the government respond to the protest?'

Zhigang smiled. 'That's a very interesting story.' He said the chief secretary of Heliongjiang Province essentially lied, claiming at a press conference that the mining problems had been addressed and the matter resolved. 'After this media report, people went out onto the streets because it meant there was no hope of sorting out the issue. This is a problem for the future. The communists believe that at the moment there is a legitimacy that's built on economic development. That's the risky side of China.'

Zhigang and I were both born in 1976, yet we had learned different things about the world when we were kids in the 1980s. Zhigang told me they never talk about the Cultural Revolution in schools. In the 1980s there was a generation of writers who wrote about the Cultural Revolution; he had to read about it in their novels. 'You never know whether school history lessons are true or fake. You need to figure it out by yourself when you grow up,' Zhigang laughed. 'The Great Firewall. It's difficult, especially for the young generation or people who don't read very much. I think they just don't care. They have good consumption, they have money, they go abroad to travel, they take Western-style food.'

China, I remarked, is the only dictatorship I can think of that looks after its people in terms of providing infrastructure. I wished Nigerian governments did the same.

'Let me ask you something,' Zhigang said. 'Where does the legitimacy of the Nigerian government come from? Why do people take this government seriously?'

There was a vote, I replied. 'It's the reverse of China. You don't have elections but the government looks after you in some way. We have elections but the government doesn't look after us.'

Zhigang looked quizzical. 'If I'm a Nigerian citizen I pay tax for the government, right? Then I vote for a government . . . what will this government do for me?'

I told him tax collection in Nigeria is not as good as it should be, though they've made improvements in the city of Lagos. 'You pay tax and electricity bills etc., yet you get little in return. People are used to it but they are angry. But what can you do? You're dealing with a government that just doesn't care.'

'Nigerians, you have democracy so it means you are not so brainwashed. In China, when you are at primary school it is very strong. We say, you have to love your country, to adore the culture, the achievement of your country.'

'That has benefits,' I countered. 'At least you believe in

one China. A politician from Guangzhou will build infra-structure for people in Heilongjiang. In Nigeria, a person from one end of the country will look at someone like me and think we are completely different peoples. There's not enough cohesion. Where does China get its collective sense of state-building?' I asked.

'To my understanding,' Zhigang replied, 'when China entered so-called "modern times" after the Qing dynasty, it was trying to learn from the West – the UK, US and France. We also try to study Japan and Russia and follow their route. So that's the origins of Chinese new ideas to build a state. They followed a complicated route – Western democracy and authoritarian regimes. All these ideas flow in the Chinese drive to build a modern nation. There were several decades of exploration – even the Cultural Revolution is part of that effort to become a modern country. Of course, the term "modernisation" is problematic. Our generation is very concerned with modernisation. The four aims – industry, science and technology, agriculture, and national defence – have been put very deeply into my generation, to our feeling about our country.'

Nigerian leaders don't think that way, I told Zhigang. There's no competitive sentiment or sense of embarrassment at failure. They tap into the globalised services to meet their personal needs. What happens to the rest of the country is not their concern.

'On the China side, it is my understanding that they want China to regain its glories, or maybe it's just a fake cover for corrupt government officials and powerholders to gain legitimacy and make a fortune. It's somehow the same.'

I disagreed. 'No, there's a big difference. I came to Wuhan from Guangzhou, one thousand kilometres on a train. A beautiful, clean train in three hours and forty-five minutes. I get on the metro here. It's clean, it works. You don't have any of that in Nigeria. We don't have a train system. We used to have one and then it fell into disrepair. The Chinese are building one line between Lagos and Abuja. That's it. Our infrastructure is terrible. That is one of the main reasons why Africans came here.'

'Is it a problem with the leaders or the institution?'

There were several reasons. When I told Zhigang that obligation to family spurs corruption, he laughed and said the Chinese have those same obligations. 'The relation of the whole family, the big family is very close.'

'Yeah, but you don't have five wives, right? You have small families!'

Zhigang chuckled.

'Our main problem,' I continued, 'is that we don't have a strong manufacturing base. Without that we rely on oil. And it becomes desperate when you've got nothing else.'

'It is very problematic. In northern China they are so dependent on mining. Coal mining.'

'But on the whole your manufacturing is amazing. That's what we lack.' When I mentioned that Nigeria is only sixty years old and needed time to get on its feet, Zhigang's response was that China is young too.

'1949,' he said.

'But you've been a state since the Han dynasty. You've had a thousand years of practice.'

'The country is always changing,' Zhigang said. 'China is actually a cultural empire.' Western provinces such as Yunnan have flitted in and out of China under various rules and regimes, he said.

But the eastern half of China has been one country for 1,000 years, I countered. 'You're ahead of us in that sense.'

'You're right,' Zhigang nodded. 'And that's the culture. Chinese culture is very strong.'

'How do you make that happen? Why would people in Guangzhou answer to someone in Beijing two thousand miles away during the Tang dynasty, for example?'

'To my understanding it is certain technologies. The first one is language. The writing was already very developed in ancient times. We can even read it still. This makes for cultural integration. Whether you're in Beijing or Hong Kong, you can read the same thing and understand each other. Also, in Beijing the bureaucratic system was well developed. Normally, after a civil servant went to Beijing to become a high-level government official, they retired and went back to their hometown or village to become a teacher or a local leader, to maintain their local community. This also maintained a linkage with central government, politically and culturally. It was a very developed system. Even the Qin dynasty, before the Han, it was already working in this way.'

'As a Nigerian I look at China . . . I want to understand how China did what it did and see how we can apply it to Nigeria. You have all these ethnic groups yet somehow you all consider yourselves Chinese.'

'Around ten years ago, economists and sociologists talked about the Chinese model. The institutional regime of China is somehow important. It's like a game. Local officials compete against each other to make business, to build infrastructure, to develop the local economy if they want to get promotion. It's an incentive for the officials to build infrastructure. Some Chinese officials went abroad to collect investors, to try to persuade people to come to China and invest. It's like Hubei Province competing against Guangdong Province. The provinces make separate deals with foreign countries. That's the economists' explanation. They've been doing this since the market reforms of the 1970s.'

That same ethos applied within the university system. As dean of his school, Zhigang is contractually obligated to double its income in the coming five years, and double the number of research papers published. It means he has to publish between six and eight personal research papers internationally during those five years. Then he will receive an evaluation. 'Also,' he added, 'the whole school votes on whether they find you satisfactory or not satisfactory.'

That's what I call pressure.

It's the polar opposite in Nigeria, where a lack of professional pride among much of our leadership allows incompetence to exist without shame. British colonialists have a lot to answer for. They deliberately overlooked the first generation of 'uppity' educated Black people (who had the 'temerity' to challenge unfair colonial policies) and handed over political power to barely literate local chiefs. Perhaps because Nigeria was created after the industrial revolution it was easier for our leaders to become rent seekers. Not being surrounded by industrialised countries didn't help matters either.

Zhigang identified with my latter observation. The Chinese government feels historically threatened by their neighbours, he said, especially Russia and Japan. China wants to keep up with them and protect itself. I hadn't viewed China in this way before. Now that I thought of it, Beijing was very preoccupied with its neighbours. I had seen constant reminders of what the Japanese did to China during the Second World War. 'Rape of Nanjing' look-backs were everywhere – on television, in gallery exhibitions. Perhaps it was a superpower with a vestigial underdog mentality.

The Communist Party's iron rule appealed to many of the Africans I'd spoken to in Guangzhou. They pined for that style of governance in their own countries – governance that built infrastructure, laid down the law and focused on poverty alleviation. China's human rights record is appalling, yes. But with people dying or suffering all the same in Nigeria and other countries, some saw little distinction between government neglect and government persecution.

Before leaving Wuhan I explored the city a little more. On the way back from the Botanical Garden the bus trundled along a causeway that traversed one of the city's many lakes and reached a set of boardwalks stretching out over the waves. I disembarked and walked along them. Groups of young people sat on the zigzagging wooden planks, laughing, chatting, canoodling. The twilight sun turned the lake an electric blue, and in the distance the colourful skyscrapers twinkled. In that moment I fell in love with Wuhan. I'd only been in the city forty-eight hours but some places just grab you.

On the final leg of my travels, I visited Xi'an, Suzhou and Shanghai. I also spent a day in the city of Yiwu, in Zhejiang Province, not far from Shanghai. It is home to the largest primary wholesale market complex in the world. I wanted to see where so many Africans obtain their export goods.

The corridor of the Yiwu International Trade City stretched endlessly ahead of me to the horizon. Four million square metres of shiny white floors.

'Where is the African products section?' I asked an Indian man.

'It's about three kilometres away,' he informed me.

I gasped.

'Good exercise!' he smiled, and waved me on.

I trekked past an unending line of wholesale shopping spaces, each around twenty-five square metres in size. There are 75,000 such outlets in Yiwu, each filled exclusively with a single product. One space contained nothing but padlocks, piled from floor to ceiling. Another shop comprised dozens of identical kerosene lamps. The next outlet displayed a plethora of binoculars while another one sold tons of dice. It was a surreal window-shopping experience. Stacks of calculators . . . scissors . . . electric fly swatters . . . glue sticks. There was a mesmeric quality to these bulk displays. Seeing two hundred padlocks dangling like Warholian art installations brought out an unexpected acquisitiveness in me. I was dying to buy stuff. Each unit was ridiculously cheap. Twenty cents for one hairbrush, I was told. 'But you must buy one thousand, minimum.' Wholesale – I kept forgetting about that. Stuffed toys, electric cars for small children gleamed. It went on and on. I must have walked for about an hour, and yet the corridor's end came no closer. Birdcages . . . 'I Love Syria' ashtrays . . . miniature Eiffel Towers . . . batteries. And as if to confirm the complex's capitalist zeal, a shop was even selling the national flags of Taiwan, China's 'renegade province'.

After two hours of walking, the immensity of this market

frazzled my eyes and bore down on my conscience. So much inorganic material, bought and consumed on a whim. We knowingly consume our own waste, like pigs eating their own shit. One day, after some future global apocalypse, people will look back and baulk at how we ceded arable soil to make plastic flowers and toys destined for landfill. For now, though, the reasoning is logical: the dictatorial government's legitimacy rests on the economic growth that will bring people out of rural poverty.

—

Beijing. City of the north. The final leg of my trip before returning to Guangzhou. The city had changed a huge amount since my parents visited in 1981. Now it was ultra-modern, and I wished that I had come here before the big changes. In her biography *Once Upon a Time in the East*, the artist Xiaolu Guo describes how art students in some neighbourhoods of Beijing slaughtered free-roaming goats and ate them. This was in the mid-1990s, around the time when I was starting university in London. The scenario described by Guo seemed unimaginable to me as I roamed the city's wide boulevards and its Dashanzi Art District. The Chinese reputation for building infrastructure at super high speed is manifested clearly here in the capital city.

Its *hutongs* (alleys lined with traditional courtyard homes known as *siheyuan*) have been gradually demolished over the decades to make way for modern buildings. Preparations for the 2008 Olympic Games hastened their demise. It was a tragedy. Even so, I couldn't help slightly envying China's transformation. Its high-speed train system, all 28,000 kilometres of it, was completed within a decade. Compare that to the UK, which, due to concerns over property and individual human rights, has agonised for twenty years over whether to build a 100-mile track between London and Birmingham. Little is sacred in China's quest for infrastructural renewal. Its lightning-speed transformation has created huge social upheaval, a process I unexpectedly witnessed first-hand in Beijing.

On my first evening in the city, I walked along the street outside my hotel, buying fruit from a grocery store, dropping off my clothes at a laundrette, and peering through restaurant windows. It was an ordinary and reasonably quiet street. The next morning, however, I woke up to the din of pneumatic drills and plumes of dust. The same street was now overrun by a cohort of construction workers who had already dismantled half of the shop fronts. The brickwork was all gone. As the workers toiled with a certain urgency, they were monitored by black-uniformed 'teqin' police-cum-security men and a crowd of curious bystanders.

Confused, I walked on and headed to the Forbidden City. Four hours later, I returned to the same street to have lunch. I was in a restaurant on the Nanheyan Road, tucking in to a lunch of shredded pork and pak choi. Towards the end of my meal, a man – presumably a government official – entered the premises alongside a policewoman. In hushed tones, the official appeared to be informing the restaurant owner of the changes that were to be made to the restaurant's architecture. As the official gesticulated at the building's façade and doorways, the manager nodded unhappily, head bowed in resignation. Dust from the neighbouring building floated outside the windows.

I was still picking pak choi from my teeth when I heard loud bangs and power drills behind me. Swivelling around, I saw two construction workers dismantling the restaurant's front entrance. Their activity threw up a torrent of grit that was clearly visible in the rays of sunlight streaming through the windows. The dust descended towards the plates of the customers still eating. I couldn't quite believe what was happening.

Quickly, I paid my bill and made for the exit, only to discover that the glass door I had used forty minutes earlier to enter the premises was now gone. Two construction workers were ripping out the doorframe and drilling away, spewing a fountain of sparks. I edged past gingerly, expecting them to pause for my safety. They didn't. They laboured hurriedly, under the steely watch of several armed policemen standing on the pavement outside. I joined the crowd of bystanders and tried to take photos of it all, but an officer in plain clothes ordered me to desist. When I asked him what was going on he motioned with anxious eyes for me to keep quiet.

By now the façades of nearly every shop on the lower end of the street had been changed in less than twelve hours. Their large windows were destroyed, covered up with bricks, and a significantly smaller window inserted much higher up. The effect was to anonymise the buildings, strip them of character and make their signage and displays redundant. One grocery store stuck out as a particularly sad case. It was the type of outlet where the till faces directly onto the street through an open window. The proprietors, a middle-aged man and woman, stood dumbstruck behind their till as the new set of bricks gradually piled up in front of them. The speed of the work was shocking yet perversely impressive (British workers never did things this fast). Such briskness came at a price, however: on closer inspection I could see that the mortaring was slapdash.

I had just witnessed the fragility of property rights in China, which are a fraught political issue right now. There was no one who could explain to me why the government was making changes to these buildings. Under Chinese property law, there is no privately held land; 'urban land' is owned by the state, which grants land rights for a set number of years. Governments can legally expropriate land for the (loosely defined) 'public benefit' and sell it on the market for a profit – up to forty times higher. The evictees don't see much of that share. Land sales are consequently a big source of revenue for local government. The sales sometimes result in civic benefits like wider roads, and fresh railway lines. But sometimes it is simply driven by corrupt government officials and their property-developer cronies.

Forced evictions are common. Protests and unrest happen from time to time, and resisters face detention, beatings, harassment. It perhaps explained the police presence near my hotel in Beijing.

In the run-up to the 2008 Beijing Olympics, many of the city's traditional hutong neighbourhoods were torn down and replaced with new developments and infrastructure projects. Housing rights organisations estimate that 1.5 million people were forced out of their homes, often with inadequate compensation.

In his book *Street of Eternal Happiness*, the journalist Rob Schmitz recounts the story of a man he met in Shanghai who refused to leave his home although it had been designated for demolition. The property developers hired thugs to get him out. They tried all sorts: cutting the water and gas supply, throwing rocks through his windows and pouring buckets of raw sewage into his home. He still didn't budge. One evening, they brought in an excavator to destroy the man's roof while he was relaxing in his living room. Falling lumber and plaster nearly crushed him. When heavy rainfall soaked his furniture, he finally gave up and left.

Chinese government authoritarianism was not the sort of leadership I would wish to live under, but such dictatorship came in handy on occasion. During the COVID-19 virus outbreak of 2019–20, the government placed the city of Wuhan into lockdown in order to halt the contagion. At the time it seemed a draconian measure to many Brits, who viewed it as one of those Chinese idiosyncrasies.

Yet three months later Britain put its cities into lockdown too, although it was too late to prevent a huge spike in hospitalisations and deaths. For all its freedoms of individuality, the UK ended up in the same position as China. The two may converge again in the future in terms of over-consumption, environmental destruction, and ageing populations. Was it better to live under a laissez-faire democratic government that reacts to calamity, or an authoritarian Chinese government that pre-empts it? The latter has its appeal. Why be bullied by circumstance into dealing with disaster, when you can be bullied by government into mitigating it? Then again, if we are all destined for catastrophe anyway, then I'd rather enjoy some freedom along the way. As someone once said, it's the *journey* that counts, not the destination.

—

The bulldozing of the façades on Nanheyan Road got me thinking about sacrifice and individual liberties. Chinese government rule is underpinned by the teachings of the ancient philosopher Confucius who believed leaders must rule society as if they were a parent. Which is quite apposite for Communist Party rule: parents – especially the old-school kind – impose curfews, they control your food supply; they force you to perform unpaid labour and they burst into your room without permission; they withhold vaccinations if they see fit; they make you up sticks and change address at their command; they punish you for any backtalk and dismiss all criticism on the basis that they gave you life. But, they insist, you'll thank them one day. To be a child is, in essence, to be robbed of your basic human agency. It is the rent we pay for protection and nurturing.

China's government justifies its trampling of human rights in its pursuit of economic growth on the basis of *chi ku* ('eating bitter'), the concept of swallowing present hardship for future gain. The factory workers spending months away from rural families, working sixteen hours a day, seven days a week for tiny salaries, lost their human rights just like the British once did during their Industrial Revolution. Rural villages devoured, families disrupted, manual jobs lost so that I, three centuries later, can order a food delivery on a cellular device. I'm grateful. Yet the Western individualist in me shudders at the thought of sacrificing my own life for the material benefit of random human beings of the future. There's only one 'me', with only one chance at this life. Utilitarianism is too hard a pill to swallow when we are each valued and unique souls.

I look at the Chinese and Africans' weaker sense of individualism with envy. Both cultures are quite similar in that respect. While Chinese culture is underpinned by Confucian philosophy, sub-Saharan African culture is underpinned by Ubuntu, the sense of social obligation and personal sacrifice; the spirit of wholeness, where 'I am you and you are me'. A precise definition of Ubuntu is hard to pin down – ask five people and you'll get seven slightly varying responses. But in essence it promotes the idea of sharing and distributing wealth in the interests of group prosperity. Though a southern African word, it is a moral philosophy that applies broadly to many of sub-Saharan Africa's hundreds of ethnic groups, at least in a pre-Christian, pre-colonial age.

Ubuntu values harmonious relationships and solidarity, rooted in the farming days to save individuals when their harvests fell through. *He who walks alone walks fastest but not the furthest.* It is similar to Confucianism in other ways. Both philosophies construct moral hierarchies based on age, with the idea that the elderly should be accorded greater respect based on the assumption that they have developed a moral wisdom that is absent in young people. And multi-party democracy sits uncomfortably with both traditions.

They both believe that living a morally good life involves, first and foremost, having rich social relations within a community. This may seem prevalent throughout the world, but it's actually distinct from other influential traditions. For example, Buddhism suggests that people should sever social attachments that cause suffering so that the individual can pursue nirvana. In Christianity, it's all about one's personal relationship with God, and having relationships with people who feel the same way. Academic Daniel Bell says that under Kantian liberalism, which informs much of northern European culture, it is 'morally acceptable for an individual to lead a lifestyle without substantial human interaction, so long as one respects other people's rights; there is no moral difference, so to speak, between somebody who has rich social ties and somebody who seeks the good in, say, technology.'

In Ubuntu, says Nigerian philosopher Segun Gbadegesin, 'every member is expected to consider him/herself an integral part of the whole and to play an appropriate role towards achieving the good of all'. Confucianism is similar, but expresses itself in different ways. While traditional sub-Saharan communities have one heart and common purpose, Confucianism recognises different types of networks, including the family, the state and then the whole world – probably as a result of China's ancient complexity and geographical vastness as a civilisation. Within Confucianism there have been debates across the centuries about whether one should put family ties above loyalty to the state in times of conflict. And while Confucians are happy to extend care for outsiders beyond their family, caring for complete strangers isn't emphasised in their moral realm, whereas Africans feel naturally obliged to give food and shelter to a complete stranger.

Africans also don't strive to 'save face', i.e. maintaining respectable facades, to the extent that the Chinese do. For the latter, sub-surface maelstroms must not ripple the surface of wider society. The writer Charlotte Ikels illustrates this in her book *The Return of the God of Wealth* in which she relays an incident where a cyclist crashes into a car and damages its taillights. An argument ensues. Passersby intervene and order the two parties to settle the dispute financially, with the cyclist having to cough up a month's salary. 'Ad hoc dispute resolution,' Ikel writes, 'focuses on the need to restore public order rather than on strict determination of guilt or innocence [. . .] Accused parties, even when guilty, know they are more likely to win support if they appear "calm, misunderstood and contrite".'

That definitely wouldn't wash in Nigeria. But I do see a similarity in our sense of social obligation and personal sacrifice at the more molecular village and family level. Historians like Michael Onyebuchi Eze say that this ideal of 'collective responsibility' is not utilitarian in placing society's wellbeing above that of the individual. Rather than the Maoist ideal of proletarian, Zhongshan-suited, one-China unity, Ubuntu is more about affirming one's humanity through recognition of an 'other' in his or her uniqueness and difference.

However, both philosophies share values of self-sacrifice and filial obligation, albeit in typically opposite ways. Time and time again I watched sibling-less Chinese kids being doted on by their fathers, grandparents and well-rested mothers. China's one-child policy began in 1980 in order to curb the growth of a population that had already hit one billion that year. Only rural families and non-Han ethnic groups were allowed to have two, although there were exceptions if both parents were only children. Boys were generally favoured, which raised rates of female infanticide, abortion and abandonment, and it created a huge gender imbalance – there are 30 million more men than women. Many of these surplus males come from rural areas, with few prospects of earning good salaries in the cities, let alone bagging a wife. It's been said to account for a one-third increase in the national crime rate, and that the intense financial pressure on men to find a partner makes them more likely to engage in criminal activities such as kidnapping and sex trafficking. The laws of supply and demand have caused 'bride prices' to surge.

Children raised without siblings, cousins or aunts, were thought to lack proper social skills, although studies came to varying conclusions on that. But what it undoubtedly did was to alter the demographic structure of the country. According to *CBC News*, the United Nations forecasts that 'China will lose 67 million working-age people by 2030, while simultaneously doubling the number of elderly.' By 2050, one-third of the country will be aged sixty years or older, with fewer workers supporting each retired person. In light of this worrying possibility, the government ended the one-child policy in 2015, and all couples were allowed to have two children. In 2021, they were allowed to have three, but within months of this new law all limits were removed. Interestingly, this hasn't triggered a rise in birth rates.

The Chinese family tree hangs like an inverse triangle, its broad ancestral roots narrowing to a single shoot (a phenomenon known as the '4-2-1 problem'). To my African eyes so many ancestors for one grandchild was a weird sight – an only child getting so much love and intensely focused attention and, I would imagine, way more edible treats than I ever did. But such a beautiful safety net might snare him or her in its tangle of emotional and financial obligation decades down the line.

For us Africans the ratio of grandparents to grandchildren is the reverse of the Chinese situation, yet it creates a similar abundance of love mixed with chafing duties. My paternal grandfather had six wives. He and my grandmother alone had six children and begat at least thirty grandchildren (when I get social-media contact requests from people claiming to be a half-cousin, I sometimes have to take their word for it). Like any large family, there is the fun of sibling companionship, a variety of relatives' homes to stay in over the holidays. And there are big family dramas: polygamy, financial infighting; children forced to play parent to their younger siblings when a parent dies.

While the Beijing government was telling its citizens to curb their breeding in the '80s onwards, Nigerians (divided loosely into Muslim north and Christian south) were obeying 'God's will' to 'multiply', raising the population from 100 million in the 1960s to more than 220 million in 2022 in an economy that has not expanded enough to accommodate everyone comfortably. The country is filled with youthful energy that sits like a powder keg, ready to ignite explosive unrest or explosive economic growth, depending on how well the government manages things in the next couple of decades.

It's funny how both societies faced worrying futures but came at a solution from polar opposite directions. Once again, so different yet so similar.

X

DRAGON'S HEAD,
SNAKE'S TAIL

'Racism in the West, the way people like me experience it, is more like a gaping injury,' said Koffi, a Ghanaian cardiovascular surgeon and invasive cardiologist who once worked in a hospital in northern China. 'It's like a gaping trauma. An open injury. You would attempt as a surgeon to try to put sutures and approximate the ends, so that you see a linear healing, but you still know there's scarring. What happens in the oriental space . . . it is a closed trauma, like a closed injury and there is nothing to suture . . . there's nowhere your needle should enter the skin, and the sutures will not need to hold anything. It's much more like lots of ants crawling on your skin. They don't bite you – they're just crawling everywhere. So that very discomfort kills you.'

'You mean Chinese racism is worse than Western racism?' I asked.

'It is millions of ants crawling everywhere on your skin!' Koffi grew animated. 'They are not biting you. Unlike the feeling of a dog bite where the canine teeth entered here . . . so you can trace it. You don't see it, you just feel it. Everything crawling on your skin.'

Koffi was chatting to me online, via Skype, from a friend's sunny garden in New England. He had spent almost a decade in China, working at a hospital in the north, but then he quit China. Although a massive Asiaphile, Koffi left with a sour taste in his mouth. He had had enough. Now he was doing a masters in global cardiac surgery in the United States and had connected with me on a professional website. When I saw his China experience I asked him if we could have a chat.

He was stocky, with a broad nose and broad shoulders, short hair, his dark skin offsetting his red shirt beautifully. Life for him had begun humbly. An only child and orphan, he was raised by his great-grandmother in rural Ghana. To pay his school fees as a boy, he would join his fisherman step-grandfather and catch fish first thing in the morning before walking ten kilometres barefoot to attend school. As a student in Accra, Ghana, he joined the International Youth Fellowship (IYF), a Korean Christian organisation that held exchange programmes. 'The oriental world was calling,' he said. But a subsequent trip to South Korea contained an ugly revelation. He claimed that the Korean students he once hosted turned out to be miscreants who had been sent to Ghana to regain some perspective. Once back in Korea, Koffi said, they gave scathing testimonies of their time in the West African country.

'I sensed that they despised everything African.' The IYF, Koffi believed, was a cover for the Korean government to get closer to Ghana's government. 'That made me change my mind about Korea.'

Koffi switched his focus to China after being blown away by the opening ceremony of the Beijing 2008 Olympic

Games. He was admitted to a university in Beijing and began studying medicine after an intense immersion course on Chinese culture, language, history and geography. (He can now give medical lectures in Chinese.) When Koffi passed the Chinese national exams some Chinese staff were surprised.

'Deep down, they don't believe Black people are intelligent,' he told me. 'The way they compliment you after you've done something tells you that they never believed.'

'What kind of things did they say?'

'We never know that you people can do that . . .'

I laughed. 'Wow, that's frank. How exactly do they phrase it?'

Koffi explained the workings of the Chinese language.

'In English we combine phonation with logical reasoning. In my mind, I'm hearing sound. And I'm making meaning in the Chinese language. When somebody speaks to you in Chinese you experience three things: you hear sound, you see pictures in your mind and you make meaning. The Chinese writing system has two parallel elements: they have pinyin and then you have the characters: pictographic, ideographic, logical aggregate and determinative phonetics. So you know that whatever they are saying you can see what pictures and images represent the words they are saying.'

'So when they say, "We didn't think you were capable of doing this", what picture comes up in your head?' I asked.

'Stupid . . . you stupid. That's the picture you see. And that's what it means.'

We both laughed incredulously.

When Koffi began practising medicine, his patients were mostly Chinese. They would see him in the outpatient clinic and then he would refer the patients to his superior. But if they were admitted to surgery Koffi had to tend to them in a more involved way.

'They see a Black person and they say no, they don't want to talk to a Black person. The patients, they have rights. They can ask for who they want to attend to them. They would say, "I don't want a Black person to touch me." And sometimes they will be discussing it in Chinese. So your curse is the fact that you understand Chinese! And their misfortune is that they don't know that you understand Chinese. So when you have all those conversations and they come into the consulting room and they realise that they were saying something bad about a person who is in charge of their surgery, there's remorse. They will be asking, "So who is going to do the surgery?" I tell them, "I'm in charge of your case."' We both chuckled. 'They would have a Chinese doctor attending to them, and then the Chinese doctor will say [Koffi speaks Chinese] "For this condition I would like to invite my colleague because he knows more . . ."'

'The patient will hear the Chinese doctor tell them, "This guy has had experience outside what we know here and knows what we know too. And I need him to do this so . . ." Some of them really do understand. That's something I like about the Chinese. They respect knowledge. They are very meritocratic in a way. That's the reason why they are submissive towards authority. So some of the patients think, "The skin is staring at me right in the face but the mind that I'm experiencing based on interaction is a bit superior and I think I'll need to submit."'

It was obvious to me that Koffi was smart. Every now and then he would say a word or sentence in Mandarin, spoken with a fabulous Chinese accent. Speaking English gave him an advantage because it enabled him to look up American, African and European guidelines immediately. He said the hospital nurses would consult him about medical ethics. 'They'll come to you, telling you, "This is what our boss says should be done. Do you think that is the same thing that would be done in America?"'

The nurses don't have access to Chinese journals, Koffi told me. According to him the journals are translated by people in government in such a way that it stops readers from thinking outside the box. No matter how well he performed, Koffi was reminded of his status as an African.

'The way they talk to you . . . the way the system works. You know that this is not a space for you. They let you know that you don't have a place here.'

'How? Give me an example.'

'For instance, my locker where you scrub and change before you go to the operating room. Opposite my locker is a picture of an African child. The famous African child with the vulture standing close by.' He was referring to the well-known photo, by South African photojournalist Kevin Carter, of a small and skeletal Sudanese child during the 1993 famine, bent over and close to death, a vulture waiting in the background. It is a haunting and heartbreaking shot. 'That picture greeted me every morning.' Koffi shook his head. 'It's an administrative thing. You can't have a say because everything is controlled by someone high up. You either see it or close your eyes.'

We could only guess at the intentions of the person who selected that photo. It might have been a gauche attempt at empathy. For us foreigners it is hard to tell where blunt ignorance ends and carefully curated racism begins in China.

'So at the end of the day, you discover that the system is programmed for you to hate where you come from,' Koffi continued, 'to hate yourself. Everything about you is wrong in China. No foreigner is right in China. That means if you get to the street and a Chinese person slaps you, *you* will be the one deported. You're an alien. You don't have any legal counsel.

'A lot of our people disappear. They arrest them and they will never be seen again. A lot of our people.' He cited those who teach English in small, remote villages. Picked up by the police, never to be heard of again (not that I could find any official evidence to corroborate this).

Koffi said he could have continued making good money if he had wanted to as a surgeon in Beijing, but the physical and material benefits did not suffice.

'Did you form close friendships with Chinese people?' I asked him.

'I have found friends. The "banana Chinese", they are the ones who know that the world is not just the little world we find ourselves in, but an ocean. They come with humility. They are genuinely interested in learning from you.' By 'banana', he meant Chinese people who were 'white on the inside' – in other words, more internationally exposed. Although considered a derogatory term by some, Koffi used it in a positive sense. He said he had grown close to his boss in the cardiac surgery unit. The man became his mentor, sometimes introducing Koffi to people as his 'teacher'.

'He became one of my friends,' Koffi told me. 'He studied at Yale. He needed someone that he could communicate with. He was very nice.'

Koffi once flew with his boss, the president of the hospital, to a conference on a first-class ticket. However, the airline stewardess refused to let Koffi take his seat and reassigned it to someone else instead. When Koffi's boss found out, he was livid. 'That was the first time I saw him in public insulting someone in Chinese!' Koffi was reinstated in his original seat in first class.

What about his experience on the dating scene?

'Their ladies are very much interested in intelligent people. You will find a Chinese person who will want to have a date with you and the husband. They will say, "I want to have a date with you but I think my husband will not allow it so I'm going to make it so that he should also come and listen to you, and I'll tell him to bring a book when he comes."'

'Huh?' I was confused.

'She will insinuate that she wants to sleep with you,' Koffi explained, 'but she will also want to tell the husband to come and see you . . . because of meritocracy, a person can literally compare you to the husband. Right in the husband's face.'

I was incredulous. 'What? What?!'

'Yes. She'll tell the husband that I am the sort of person she should be married to.'

I laughed.

'No joke. And sometimes they go as far as to say to their husband, "I am telling you so that in case you ask me where I am and I tell you that I'm with this person, you will know what I am talking about."'

'Is this just one person who did this? Or are you generalising?'

'No, you have lots of people who do this. Literally lots of people do this.'

'And how do the husbands react? What does the husband say?'

'There's something about Chinese society that lots of people don't know,' Koffi said. 'Marriage in China is much more like a contract. More like buying a wife. And because of that maltreatment that the women are experiencing . . . who the man marries is probably not a decision made by the man himself, and the house they live in is bought for him, probably by the parents.' The gender imbalance created by China's former one-child policy leaves Chinese parents feeling obliged to marry off their sons with even greater urgency than before. They'll agree the bride price, cover the marriage costs and provide a wedding apartment or house, or face shame from society and their ancestors. For these parents, accumulating money becomes vital for boosting their sons' competitiveness in the marriage market.

'Some of the women begin to interact with foreigners and see the difference . . . The women feel that once they're working and can make money . . . it's a feminine society . . . The guy will become friends with her and her husband. "My wife is always talking about you." The husband will tell the guy, "What have you said to her? She's really changed." Most of them will say she's changed for good. Because when they fall for you, they fall. Eight-five per cent of Chinese are not satisfied with their marriage. The country with the highest cases of infidelity in the world is China.'

'How do you know this?'

'I have scrubbed in 10,000 surgeries in China. I have interacted with more than 200,000 people. These are people that I have physically touched, done examinations on them.

Those individuals will insinuate how they are not satisfied with their marriage.'

Patients open up to Koffi because doctors in China are traditionally more like spiritualists, who take a more holistic approach to patient care, looking after their mind and spirit.

I asked him whether he fell in love with anyone Chinese. His voice changed. He became hesitant. Something was being held back – perhaps heartbreak.

'I did not go there looking for love,' he said eventually. 'That was not my intention going there. I tried dating. I dated two Chinese women, to the point where their families said they cannot accept a Black person. But that was not the reason why it never went further. It just doesn't feel the same. I can't live there. I'm a bird in flight.' He chuckled with faint unease. 'When I went to China I was wrestling with myself. Because everything you are is "inferior". Everything about you as a person is wrong. You go to a restaurant, you go to a washroom, you go anywhere there will be someone saying something about why you can't be there. You're considered bad, you're considered criminal. Someone is always saying something.'

'Do they say it to your face?'

'Yes, they are saying it and they will deny it. When that repeats for a long, long, long time, you begin to question your judgement. It messes your head up.'

'Did it make you angry?'

He nodded. 'In China, adrenalin is the norm. I practise Buddhist dhamma. I'm a very spiritual person. I went to China with a dream. I'm grateful for everything that happened to me.'

'But . . . ?'

'People need to know it's bad the way we are treated there. I want people to know it's a lie . . . the African leadership that goes to China do not care what Africans are doing over there. They only care about the shopping they've come to do in China, the food they can eat, the young Chinese girls who come and massage them. They don't read the contracts, they just sign. If they cared about African people they could listen to the many African students who are there, who understand the language, who are experts like myself in other fields, who can give them tangible information in economics, agriculture. But they won't do that.

'They believe that the Chinese are there to help Africa,' he said. 'They don't know the narrative in China.'

'What is the narrative in China?'

'That everything in Africa is free and that all the Africans in China are being taken care of free by the Chinese government. So when you walk on the street and you dress nicely and you are eating good food that you actually work hard for, people there think they have done it for you.'

Koffi invoked a Korean proverb, 'dragon's head, snake's tail', to describe how China can seem modern on the surface, with its big new cities, but behind the metropolitan curtain lies deep rural poverty.

'Those people are living in a deplorable state. It's a big country. Every country has its challenges, but these are places that are really struggling. They are where we have our underground Christian missions. We African brothers go to give people clothes. We give them shoes and food. We go to these villages, give free programmes, medical programmes, things like that. So when the Chinese narrative is "We are going to save Africa" then you are not respected as an African. People can say anything about you and you can't say a word back.'

For all his complaints, something had obviously kept Koffi in China for close to a decade. What was it that he loved about the place?

'The food is really something. And they are very hospitable people. Someone can invite you to their home. For instance, during their Chinese New Year Spring Festival the hospital administrator or the leader of the whole company drove to my quarters and then took me to his home. He feels that you are in a far distant land and you don't have your family and relatives. Those are some of the warmest things I've experienced. For an outsider to be allowed to be present. I was considered a family friend. That was really touching. Very, very touching.

'There is a lot of brouhaha about Chinese not liking Black people, which is true to some extent. But when it's obvious that this person merits that ... they can't hide it. For instance, there's another doctor there who was the first Black person to be on a Chinese medical board, and he served as a consultant for a big sporting event. They gave him a whole front page of their newspaper when Obama was given the back page. If this were Africa, Obama would be given the big front page. "An African doctor and friend has come to handle our medical issues ..." That was really special. They have a different way of doing things. One of the best experiences.'

China's culture of hard work appealed to Koffi too. 'A city that I went to had very dilapidated communities. You go out, you go to sleep and come back the next day and a whole forest of skyscrapers is in front of you. They will put up a whole forest in just a day. Those things that I have seen changed my perspective. Some of those things can easily be done in Africa. You know, they really motivate you.'

It didn't take long for Koffi's recollections to turn sour once again, however. He recalled the day he was eating in Andi's, an African restaurant in Beijing, when the police entered the premises as part of a drugs raid.

'We had to pee in a cup in public, you know? That was the most shaming thing I have ever experienced. There was a bathroom close by but they didn't want to let you go, pee in a cup and bring it back, because they want to test for drugs. That was the day I cursed myself and said, "I'm never going to stay here".

'China is a great place. They build great stuff, magnificent structures. But when the buildings are too tall people become dwarfed in their understanding and reasoning. And when the lights are too bright, people are blinded. They can't see.

'It took the whites so many years to understand that Blacks are human beings. If the white supremacists think they are even better, then how about the yellow man? We need to give them time and space to evolve and understand who we are. Until then they will be peeing and pooing on us. But they will get there . . . they will get there.'

Koffi exemplified everything I admire about Africans abroad, and especially in China: a hardiness, tenacity, and facility for language. He had studied medicine in one of the trickiest languages on earth, practised his medicine in an intensely foreign environment, assimilating to some degree and becoming a useful bridge between Ghana and China. He was part of the first wave of immigrants, braving all the ignorance and prejudice that came with it. But I could see that it had taken a toll; his emotions were understandably raw. The rational side of his mind competed with the emotional, as he veered between even-handed assessments and piqued generalisations about the Chinese. Life in China was a psychological tightrope balancing act, and not always for the faint-hearted. He had taken one for the team; in doing so he had exposed people here to Africans, expanded their ideas of what was possible, and I loved him for that.

—

I was back in Guangzhou and grateful for it. My time in other regions of China made me realise that the attitude to foreigners in this southern city was relatively cosmopolitan. No more titters as I walked past. But I didn't feel like returning to the world of Sanyuanli and Xiaobei districts just yet. I wanted a change of scene, to have different kinds of conversation, to experience non-African Guangzhou.

Through my contacts, I ended up staying with a Chinese guy called Lixin and his Belgian husband, Nicolas. Both men were in their early thirties. Lixin designed fashion accessories. Fresh from the holiday beaches of Vietnam he was tanned, dimple-faced, taller than average, with a flamboyant dress sense that varied from long, dark Yamamoto coats to Kermit-green suits. Nicolas worked for a European engineering company. Fair-haired and slender, he was sporty and outgoing and flung himself into the river of life, letting it carry him wherever. He had even co-starred in a romantic Hong Kong Chinese-language movie.

Staying with Nicolas and Lixin was a liberating change of scene from Chocolate City. I wanted to plug into mainstream Guangzhou and nourish the art-loving, restaurant-eating part of my soul. Their apartment had stunning views of the Pearl River. The bay windows in my bedroom overlooked the river's glorious bend. The city skyscrapers sparkled after dark in a chromatic extravaganza, and Guangzhou Bridge shone with neon lights that changed colours every few seconds. Joggers, lovers and cyclists filled a riverside promenade festooned with fairy-lit trees. For this spacious crib (three bedrooms, two bathrooms, large living room and kitchen) Lixin and Nicolas paid the equivalent of £900 a month – slightly less than what I shelled out for a 200-square-foot shoebox studio in London. It was enough to make me seriously consider moving to Guangzhou permanently.

Lixin and Nicolas seemed very content here.

'Homosexuality in China is not illegal,' Lixin told me. 'People only have a problem with it when it's in their own family.'

This was something I was beginning to understand about Chinese society. Attitudes towards homosexuality here are interesting. It has never been illegal – instead it's been tolerated on a surprising scale and for a long time. In the city of Hangzhou during the Song dynasty of the thirteenth century, gay bars co-existed with other establishments along the banks of the lake. Beneath the filial piety there was a flexibility and pragmatism. His people take a roundabout route to achieve an objective, Lixin said, drawing an elliptical orbit with his finger. Everything is a means to an end.

'The government responds softly to soft criticism, but harshly to harsh criticism,' Lixin explained. It was a cultural trait a Ghanaian friend of his never got to grips with despite living in Guangzhou for ten years. When the Ghanaian vented his frustration with certain matters it created a snow-ball effect and led to clashes with people, Lixin said.

The dynamic between him and Nicolas was amusing to watch. Whatever chemistry brought them together clearly wasn't linked to politics. They disagreed often, especially on matters Hong Kong-related. Lixin – an urbane guy who wore ladies' wigs at gay pride parties – was surprisingly supportive of the national government. In contrast to Nicolas's view of Hong Kong as a beacon of freedom, Lixin disliked Hong Kongers' disdain for mainlanders. Nicolas reckoned they felt that way because of 'differences in education'. Lixin bridled at the suggestion that mainlanders weren't as educated, and he insisted that all tenants were compensated after being evicted from their homes to make way for new urban developments. He also believed that Tibet belonged to China.

'But Tibetans have their own language and culture,' I remarked.

Lixin didn't get why that should merit autonomy. I struggled to argue against him – Nigeria has hundreds of ethnic groups and languages, after all.

'What do you think of the Dalai Lama?' I asked him.

Lixin pursed his lips. 'He is dishonest. He pretends he's a spiritual leader but he's just a politician. Anti-China.'

Nicolas rolled his eyes and took out his phone. He showed me a headline he had stored from the English-language Chinese newspaper. The National Communist Party convention was taking place that day, so the government had limited internet access across the country to prevent dissent. Yet the headline said something along the lines of 'Chinese People applaud the government's internet blackout'. Nicolas laughed at the crudity of its propaganda.

Again, I put it to Lixin that the Chinese internet firewall was an infringement of human rights. 'No,' he shook his head, 'they just want us to use the Chinese version and to support Chinese companies.'

Nicolas groaned and shook his head.

—

Another night, I walked with Lixin, Nicolas and Alex, a French fashion designer who taught at a college in Guangzhou, enjoying letting them introduce me to new parts of the city. The four of us sauntered around Zhujiang New Town district. In the 1980s, this area was largely an expanse of rice paddies. The authorities then changed its name to Tianhe, the Chinese word for Milky Way, which was a fitting name since the area is now a constellation of lights and neon and skyscrapers. The Guangzhou Opera House, designed by the Iranian-British architect Zaha Hadid, dominates one end next to Zhujiang Boulevard, a sweeping expanse of concrete. At night its pavement was lit up with strips of coloured neon – red, white, pale greens and blues streaking across at angles. Neon may be a cheap trick, a passé shortcut to wonderment, but it didn't stop me wandering about wide-eyed and foolishly enchanted.

We stopped at a large hoarding with an illustration of the housing development soon to be built in the area. Landscaped gardens and mid-rise apartment blocks. The government, which owns the land, was on a massive building programme. Evictions were common, people forcibly moved out to make way for fresh housing developments. Nicolas said they were supposed to be given money to resettle elsewhere, but some people aren't compensated properly, if at all. Again, Lixin disagreed.

'They get paid good money,' he insisted tetchily.

'How much?' I asked.

'Maybe 100,000 yuan,' he replied. That's about £10,000. Nicolas tutted. I kept silent.

—

One night, Lixin and Nicolas took me to a restaurant in Food City in the Liede Subdistrict, an area full of restaurants and bars. The sign at the threshold of Food City was a direct and clunky translation: 'The Entrance of Central Business District Kitchen Food Street'.

We joined a group of Lixin and Nicolas's friends at an Indonesian restaurant. They were a young, international motley crew that included a Colombian woman who imported goods; Lixin's best friend, Juliette; Alex, and a couple of Belgian guys. I sat opposite a handsome, forty-year-old Frenchman who told me, with neither pride nor shame, that he had three girlfriends. ('One in Hong Kong, another in Shanghai and one in Tokyo.')

When it came to dating, white men had a grand old time in China. Whether hot or unattractive, they and Chinese women shared space at the top of the racial dating hierarchy. White women came next – sought after by white men and Chinese men. Chinese men are sought after by Chinese women, less so by white women. African men were desired by some Chinese women. African women were at the bottom of the pile. Thank god I wasn't looking for love. Everyone at the table explained to me that European men who like

Chinese men are called 'rice queens' while Chinese guys who prefer dating white guys are known as 'potato queens'.

I asked Alex if he dated Chinese men. 'Chinese men love with their heads not their hearts,' he replied. He had a Caribbean boyfriend back in France.

Across the table was Juliette. Belgian, a lesbian, and a designer too, she was based in Shanghai but frequently travelled to Guangzhou for work. She and Lixin were so close they pretended to Lixin's parents that they were a couple.

In fact, Lixin had married Nicolas in a ceremony in Belgium, but their union was not legally binding in China. When they travelled together, Nicolas played the role of 'best friend'. Juliette recounted the time she and Nicolas accompanied Lixin to his parents' village in Zhejiang Province, near Shanghai.

Juliette was surprised at what she saw. This was the other China: no running water, no electricity, no televisions. Choruses of rooster crows filled the air. For hot baths, his parents heated a bucket of water over a stove. This was where Lixin grew up, and for country kids like him the competition to get into university had been fierce. From age eleven he attended a nearby boarding school and concentrated hard. Only he and one other boy were selected from their village to go on to tertiary education. In the twelve years since he first attended university, Lixin had recast himself as an urbane designer with a husband and an apartment overlooking the Pearl River; beach holidays in Thailand, France, Vietnam and the Philippines; drag parties in Hong Kong. The speed of transformation was staggering.

'He doesn't talk about his childhood,' Juliette told me. She suspected he was embarrassed about it. Lixin's pro-government stance made more sense once I learned about his upbringing. The Communist Party had fulfilled its aim of giving people like him a better life, an unfettered life. Perhaps it explained why he defended the government whenever Nicolas criticised it.

When Juliette arrived at Lixin's home village, his parents welcomed her and Nicolas. They put Lixin and Juliette – 'such a charming couple' – in a tent that lacked central heating. Arctic winter air blasted through it, compelling Juliette to cuddle up to Lixin in their 'marital' bed. Meanwhile Nicolas shivered in a separate tent next door.

I couldn't stop laughing at the thought of it.

Lixin had told his sister about his sexuality and she had accepted it, but coming out to their parents was a challenge he preferred to sidestep for the time being.

—

After dinner we moved further down the street to one of the many colourful bars that opened out onto the pavement. There I encountered yet another fascinating Black immigrant – from the Bahamas this time. Jillian was a petite twenty-eight-year-old obstetrician with sensationally smooth skin and an American accent derived from a posh Bahamian high school. She had lived in Beijing – alone and without her parents – since the age of seventeen, and spoke fluent Mandarin.

Why the hell was a Bahamian woman practising obstetrics in China?

'I qualified here.'

'Yes, but why?'

Jillian said she had been 'having too much fun' as a teenager, so her mother refused to fund her degree at an American college. It was a vague response, perhaps intentionally so. I didn't probe any further. Like Koffi, Jillian gained her medical degree in the Chinese language, which was a sensational achievement. She told me that Chinese women's pelvises have shrunk significantly over the last three generations.

'Rural women's pelvises are wide because they carry heavy loads. They used to give birth in the fields unassisted, but an urban lifestyle has made them taller with narrower pelvises. Forty per cent of them have caesareans now.'

I sipped a gin and tonic and turned to look at the street. Two Black guys sashayed past, hips swinging. The skinnier one wore tight grey jeans tucked into calf-length black boots. China is supposedly a place of freedom for gay African men needing to escape the strictures and expectations of their home countries.

Our group moved on to a gay club where a 'bear' stripper was billed to perform. I didn't associate Chinese men with hirsuteness or big muscles, so I was intrigued. The club was dark, filled almost exclusively with men and choked with cigarette smoke. I watched in awe as Jillian chatted to punters in Chinese. The world was truly her oyster. Comfortable in the West and in the East, she had skills that even the most ardent racist would grudgingly appreciate.

I sat down on an L-shaped sofa and surveyed the scene. Men were chatting in pairs mainly, and sipping beers. Not a huge amount of dancing going on. The MC then intro-duced the stripper, and the crowd cheered as a buff Chinese guy appeared on the central stage, wearing a black suit, white shirt and black necktie. By global standards his beard was wispy, but by local standards he was a grizzler. Dancing and strutting around the stage, he stripped down to his thong. Lixin and I exchanged glances and chuckled. The stripper pulled down his thong and shook his bare butt cheeks to the music. But the front of his thong stayed firmly on, his cupped hands covering his unmentionables. Though I was relieved not to see a full frontal, I was still bemused by the no-show.

The crowd cheered and whistled in a manner that was more restrained than I had anticipated. Dressed in everyday jeans, T-shirts, baseball caps, one would never have guessed they were gay. Their body language gave nothing away either. That was the strange thing – no kissing, no handholding, no touching.

'The authorities will close down the club if the guys kiss or get too friendly with each other,' said the promoter, an Indonesian called DJ Squidz. China, once again, was so full of contradictions. This was a country that had no law against homosexuality and allowed a male stripper to wiggle his bare butt at a crowd of gay men. Yet if those men got too friendly with each other they risked losing their venue.

I exchanged numbers with Squidz and arranged to visit his main club, a straight one, the following weekend. There I would find an international crowd, including Africans, he said.

—

It was past 2 a.m. on a warm evening when I arrived in the Ouzhang neighbourhood. Straight-faced bouncers manned the doors, and a massive 'No to drugs' poster was erected prominently outside the building – I suspected it was more a signalling of virtue to the police rather than a warning to the clientele.

Guangzhou is sometimes called the capital of the developing world, and it showed tonight. Among the people hanging out on the sidewalk was a Russian skater dude who gave a 'wass up' to everyone. The club manager, a Russian girl, was a no-nonsense, clipboard-wielding type who persistently gave me dirty looks. A student from Côte d'Ivoire stood nearby. Dressed in a scoop-neck pink T-shirt and wearing sparkly earrings in both ears, he looked more gay than the boys at the bear club – but I guess I'm just old-fashioned. He was play-fighting with his girlfriend, a beautiful girl from New Caledonia in the Pacific. I liked the young pair's dynamic. They were a happy couple, unencumbered by the visa issues, parenthood or business worries that the Xiaobei and Sanyuanli folks contended with.

Over towards the club entrance, a collection of Indonesian, Filipina, Colombian, African and Chinese prostitutes stood with a prospective air about them, all miniskirts, bare legs, translucent heels and heavy make-up.

I got chatting to Nana, a bone-thin tomboy from Niger who wore a blonde weave. A dancer by day, she also managed the club nights. She was extroverted and confident, and being a woman in the overwhelmingly male African community didn't bother her. 'I've been like this all my life,' she told me. 'I don't want to have girlfriends because it's boring. I always find myself with boys. I love the same thing they love, everything they do.' She welcomed me into the club.

Inside, I saw a Malian guy with a gold chain and a dark, skinny face. His friend, another large Malian, wore aviator sunglasses despite the darkness and was chatting with two peroxide-blonde Eastern European women tottering on very high heels. Their pneumatic cleavages almost tilted their centre of gravity. Squidz let me sit in the VIP section on the mezzanine, near a quartet of the only Chinese people in the club. They nursed bottles of Moët and sat apart from the crowd in a spirit of either chippiness or aloofness.

I stood on the balcony by a glass cage where two scarcely dressed Eastern European women danced and shimmied to the rhythm. Down below, the Malian boys were jumping up and down on the tables, beneath fluorescent lights that made their all-white clothes dazzle in contrast to their noir complexions. I was one of only two African women in the club, and my sole age-mate was a balding, ponytailed Mediterranean man who swanned around high-fiving people. The crowd went crazy when the DJ played the Ludacris song 'Move Bitch'. I wasn't feeling the music at all. From my balcony vantage point I surveyed the dancefloor with an air of mild disdain, like those grumpy old-fart muppets, Statler and Waldorf.

It was a tacky scene and the music was terrible, but it warmed my heart to see humans of every hue coming together. The ethnic configuration, this absence of western Europeans, was fascinating. Barring the Russians I was looking at a United Nations without the Security Council. Thirty-five years ago nobody could have predicted this collection of nationalities would be dancing together freely behind the Bamboo Curtain. The world is so unpredictable. Who knows: in 2050 I could be watching North Korean and Congolese kids dancing in a Nigerian neighbourhood in Kabul.

—

One morning, back in my Sanyuanli hotel room, I woke up to a lewd text message from a Nigerian man called Prosper, who I had met the previous day. We had had dinner at Chimamanda's and I sat with him in a Chinese nail salon and watched while he treated himself to a pedicure. From my perspective it was all friendly, innocent fun. For Prosper, our half-day hangout was a *prelude*. His text was a jpeg, written by god-knows-who, that had been doing the rounds, and involved descriptions of sex acts.

When I gave him a piece of my mind in return (again via text), Prosper seemed surprised by my irritation:

'Wow, sorry' . . . 'Easy, why ur calling me idiot' . . . 'too bad' . . . 'Am sorry for dat' . . . 'Forgive and forget' . . . 'Pls'.

I never saw him again.

It was an awkward situation, being an African woman in this city and writing about men. My interest in them was open to constant misinterpretation and confusion. In Sanyuanli, I lunched sometimes at Chimamanda's Kitchen, a brightly coloured Nigerian restaurant, where the Christian reggae was loud, and the conversations even louder. I was always the only woman in there. The overwhelming maleness of the place – a few of them on the rough side – gave it an air of a prison canteen where I was the freshest meat on the menu. Diners took turns striking up conversation with me. When one conversation ended, another man would stop me for more chat or slide onto my table. And I made time for them in the hope of getting fresh gossip or interesting infor-mation. I was hanging on to their every word, enquiring about their marital status, asking for their phone numbers and arranging second meet-ups. Watching all of this was the manager, who regarded everything through half-mast eyes and an almost permanently zipped mouth, as if just yanked out of a deep sleep.

For the most part the men I spoke to were polite and accepted my rebuffs with gentlemanly grace. But after more than four months I was craving more female conversation. The women were like butterflies, rare specimens that bounced away on my approach. One day, however, someone came along and flipped the script.

Friday Prayers had finished just as I had completed lunch at the Madina restaurant in Xiaobei. Muslim Uighur men strolled down the street, looking fresh in their white robes and accompanied by their womenfolk who wore lace head-scarves and brightly coloured coats. While I stood on a street corner photographing them, a pretty African woman in a woolly hat came up to me and said hi. She was that rare thing in Xiaobei: an African woman who approached me for conversation. Her name was Suzy. Kenyan, twenty-three years old, skinny and, despite being ethnic Kikuyu, she had the big eyes, pale skin and chiselled features of an Ethiopian.

Suzy invited me to join her on her trip to a market across town. As we sat on a subway train, she told me she came from a working-class background. Her father owned a small stall selling food. Suzy had a refreshing demeanour, an open, free-spiritedness that would be unremarkable in a city like Nairobi but, in the context of African Guangzhou, was relatively unusual. I moaned about my experience of being a woman in a predominantly male community.

'If you are a lady it is not easy to be out because they all think you are like a prostitute. Those Nigerians, they say, Hey baby, and so on . . . I want your number . . . where's your hotel? They don't know how to talk to women,' she chuckled.

Xiaobei, she explained, was a red-light area. Most ladies here were on the game, which explained why I had such trouble photographing women. They were constantly recoiling from my lens in panic.

I followed Suzy to a couple of markets and chatted while she perused baby strollers, clothes and other goods to export. This was her side hustle. She operated as a buyer for customers, complete strangers who sent her text messages with their requests and gave her the money via the WeChat app; a commercial relationship based entirely on trust. Her main job was teaching English to Chinese school kids.

Africans in Guangzhou found it hard to get teaching jobs, partly because their English isn't fully up to scratch and partly because the Chinese are snobbish about who they want to learn the language from. Suzy pretended she was American in order to get her job. When they learned of her African passport they still employed her but at a reduced salary. Her pupils were kids of all ages.

'What are your students like?' I asked.

She smiled: 'They are naughty. They just talk girlfriend and boyfriend. They are very, very naughty. They ask me, "Teacher Suzy, I have a question for you. Do you have a boyfriend?" *Every day* they ask me this! They know I don't like it. It cracks me up.' The teenage boys cheekily asked her out on dates. Because she pretends she's American, they believe she has lots of boyfriends – Americanness means promiscuity, in their minds. 'Some are sixteen years old and some are in senior high school. They tell me, "Can you take me to your country? I just want to be your boyfriend,"' Suzy chuckled. 'Sometimes I ask them to construct sentences in English, using the word "never". Their answer is the same:

"*I will never have a girlfriend.*" The girls too: "*I will never have a boyfriend.*" Finish. Sometimes that's the only theme. The teachers tell me, "You don't have to worry about them. These are just teenagers, you cannot control them.'"

I had imagined Chinese school kids to be obedient automatons but, Suzy explained, extra-curricular language schools don't impose that same level of discipline. There were cultural miscommunications too, she said. Like the time when she tried teaching the kids how to say 'six'. She stuck up five fingers on her left hand and the little finger of her right hand. The kids started giggling. They explained that raising your little finger is considered a rude gesture. To my horror, I realised I had been making that same obscene gesture when bartering with people. Suzy explained that the Chinese gesture for 'six' is to ball up your fist and stick out your thumb and little finger.

We were back on the metro again. Suzy removed her woolly hat for the first time that afternoon and showed me the scar on her scalp where she had had an abscess removed in a Guangzhou hospital. 'It's healing very fast . . . I told the doctors, "You see? I don't have HIV because it has healed fast."' She smiled. 'The doctors were laughing. Because I come from Kenya they know that in Kenya we have many people that have HIV.' Suzy wasn't the first African to tell me how frankly Chinese doctors expressed their fears about African patients' HIV status.

She and I stared at a gorgeous Chinese toddler waddling past us. We both agreed that the babies here were very cute.

'The Chinese just have one kid, so for them they don't suffer,' Suzy commented. 'You know, at home if you have a baby and you take your kid to your mum you feel like you're punishing your mum. But the Chinese, once they have a baby they take it to their mum and their mum will be taking care of them. And once they have one kid – finish. They don't bother to get another one. But for us they want us to have many so they can help you! My mother had five children.'

Suzy and I parted ways and exchanged details on WeChat. She was due to return to Kenya over the Chinese New Year holidays. En route, she would do a three-day stopover in Dubai to do some sightseeing. Her job as a buyer and the teaching job gave her a financial freedom she didn't have back at home.

Later that week, I perused Suzy's photo album on her WeChat account. She was the embodiment of a free-spirited twenty-something living her best life thanks to her opportunities in China. Gone was the woolly hat and in its place was a long, wavy weave, cascading down her back. In a selfie video she flicked her hair back, pouted and stared vamp-eyed into the lens. Another photo showed her in Dubai, riding the sand dunes on a quad bike while dressed in tight jeans and a skimpy vest. I swiped to find an image of her on the beach in a tight white dress, waves cresting on her bare feet. In another photo Suzy posed demurely with her Chinese students, hair scraped back. The final photo showed her on an Emirates aircraft, playfully wearing an air stewardess's lace train pillbox hat while the stewardess grinned beside her. Caption: 'Benefits of being jovial. Can survive anywhere in the world.'

There were many Africans like Suzy, enjoying their life in China, but they were hard to prise open for conversation. Those who benefited the most from life here tended to keep a low profile, afraid to lose what they had worked hard to build. I heard about them, these old-timers who had built up successful trade businesses since the 1990s and had become millionaires. They lived in cities like Yiwu and Beijing as well as Guangzhou.

Other Nigerians came to China to play professional football in the hope that they would be spotted by European or American scouts. A number of them now coach soccer in various towns and cities across China. There are those guys living contented lives, teaching karate, teaching English, enjoying a certain ease that they hadn't found in their home countries, and certainly couldn't find in the West. It was nice to see them enjoying a sliver of the mobility enjoyed by Europeans, who could up sticks and live and work in Spain, Portugal, Sweden, Italy, Holland on a whim and make a living.

—

I was about to leave China for good. From my hotel in Sanyuanli, I took a final walk around various parts of Guangzhou, ruminating on my time in the country. I emerged from Xiaobei's subway station exit, crossed the pedestrian bridge and returned to the Tianxiu Building to peruse the merchandise on sale one last time.

I bought one item as a souvenir: Sexlove Chewing Gum. The blurb on the packaging was a fabulous paragraph of pseudoscience written in my favourite language, Chinglish: This was 'A sexuality arousing' gum, which 'has created numerous hot and beautiful girls. It can generate the uncontrollable sexual desire for girls within 10-20 minutes after taking. During the arousal period it can generate constant pleasure and climax. It is proven after clinical experiments that it can instantly strengthen the sexual desire after orally taking. Cautions: This product is only for spouse. Do not use it for other purposes.'

Dangling from a hanger were a pair of buttock-cushioned bodices, known as yansh pads. I wouldn't have expected a demand for this in Africa where flat backsides are a rarity. Then again, there are no limits to our insecurities. The Tianxiu Building is an emporium dedicated to the false betterment of African women and men: hair extensions, skin lightening creams, aphrodisiacs. The basement stalls sold human hair to be used as weaves. The hair was displayed under the region of origin: Peru, Malaysia, Brazil. It came from all over the world and was made in China for Africans to come and purchase and export for decreasing profit margins.

Outside the Tianxiu Building, I crossed the pedestrian bridge. The same moneychangers were standing there, the same disabled man spread out on the floor, the same babel of languages. But the photographer who once took portraits of Africans had now vanished. The dwindling demand she had spoken of had disappeared altogether. Her apparatus, her printer and the photographs of African immigrants hanging on a board were all gone. The wave of African immigration to China had crested.

Having spent nearly five months in China, it was clear to me that the oft-quoted figure of 200,000 Africans living in Guangzhou was an exaggeration – or at least outdated. The authorities don't count or produce official figures. The 'swamping' of China by hua gei is a notion spread by certain elements of the media and amplified in the hollows of fact-void, nativist imaginations. Educating myself required proactive effort. I had to buy academic books and research papers in order to obtain any proper analysis and information about the situation. In her book, the author Shanshan Lan writes that the provincial authorities created laws to prevent foreigners from establishing homes or offices near government or military zones. She was told in confidence by a city official that this law was created to prevent Xiaobei from expanding and turning into an African town.

But China wouldn't tolerate African immigrants at all if it didn't benefit from them in some way. It would have got rid of them by now if it wanted to. One only has to look at the treatment of the Uighurs and diasporan Chinese dissidents to know that the Communist Party is no impotent handwringer in these matters.

The reality is that Africans have boosted the local economies of Sanyuanli and Xiaobei and inspired urban renewal in an area long avoided by property developers. They created a customer base for Chinese bankers, shipping entrepreneurs, hotel owners, who could also take advantage of the undocumented folk and charge them higher prices. Chinese immigration police also made money from African immigrants, especially the undocumented ones. Armed with discretionary powers of arrest, they demand bribes from such vulnerable people. There's a vested interest in not deporting them.

Chinese landlords enjoy a slice of the pie too. Many of the original residents of Xiaobei moved away and rented their properties to Africans who generate a regular rental income for them. By law, the landlords should have registered their tenants, but many of them didn't bother. This cosy arrangement came to haunt those Africans during the 2020

COVID-19 pandemic when they became scapegoats, labelled as illegal residents and vectors of disease.

A symbiosis also exists between Africans, their Chinese landlords and shopping centre owners. The latter, on hearing of imminent police raids, are known to warn the Africans to hide, and bribe the police to be lenient on anyone they catch. In Xiaobei, some Uighurs and illegal rural migrants also have to be wary of the police, but relations between them and the cops are sensitive too and need to be maintained for political stability.

All of this had shifted my perceptions about China's leadership. It was more nuanced than I imagined. Admittedly I had been influenced by global perceptions of the Communist Party as unyielding hard-asses to be feared more than any other. The Yellow Peril. There was a lot of truth to this (within its own self-defined borders China was expansionist, aggressive and cruel, especially in the Spratly Islands, Tibet and Xinjiang Province). But when it came to China's attitude towards the rest of the world, I think I had wrongly projected onto it the expansionist, moralising zeal of Western imperialism. In the global context, China's ambition doesn't quite seem that of the American pioneer or Hitlerian lebensraum variety – it has its hands full managing its own massive population. Of course, economic expansion always runs the risk of mission creep that results in something resembling a form of colonialism.

Chinese domestic rule had two faces. An obvious bluntness, yes, but also a subtlety I hadn't appreciated. It called to mind the famous proverb by the ancient philosopher Lao Tzu, whose Taoist beliefs underpin part of modern China's psyche:

Water is fluid, soft, and yielding. But water will wear away rock, which is rigid and cannot yield. As a rule, whatever is fluid, soft, and yielding will overcome whatever is rigid and hard. This is another paradox: what is soft is strong.

The Chinese ruling party had to tread carefully with Africa where some of their own Chinese immigrants are behaving badly. The pangolin trade is a case in point. Some Chinese (and other Asian nationalities) believe that the scales of these anteaters are good for one's health, and so demand for them has risen. Organised criminal syndicates have set up trafficking networks in Nigeria, and can earn up to US$250 for the scales from one pangolin. Just as with drug dealing in Guangzhou, this illegal trade relies on cooperation between locals and the immigrants. Bushmeat hunters in Nigeria are hunting the animals so zealously they are becoming harder to find in the forest.

Chinese demand for Nigerian commodities affects society in other ways. A friend of mine who lives in Nigeria's capital city, Abuja, told me the iron grills covering the city's street drains have been removed by thieves who smelt the metal and sell it to the Chinese. Chinese illegal activities had grown so much that an employee at the Chinese Embassy in Lagos told Shanhan Lan that when President Xi visited Nigeria he paid specific attention to the country's problem with *san fei* Chinese (those who enter, stay or work illegally), and asked the matter to be dealt with cautiously. African leaders were also vocal in their criticism when Nigerian residents in Guangzhou were unfairly targeted and evicted during the COVID-19 pandemic. Beijing's ambassador in Abuja was summoned to a meeting with the Nigerian leadership.

Beijing, knowing that it has san fei problems, must listen and tread carefully. China has done some good things in Africa, but as with any story, there's a flip side.

After spending time in China, it was more obvious than ever that Africans' future here was precarious. Most people I'd met weren't hell bent on spending the rest of their lives here, they simply have the basic human desire to live, survive and thrive wherever they can. Migrating to China without knowing a soul seemed to me an act of incredible bravery. But Ikem, the jeweller in Sanyuanli, disagreed.

'Nigeria is a place of darkness,' he once told me. He found scant comfort in that country, with its 250 ethnic groups, where moving fifty kilometres in any direction can render you a foreigner anyway. Trying to make it in Guangzhou was no less daunting to him than hustling in Lagos or any other city in Nigeria.

—

Even during my short time in China, there was a sense that the African community was shrinking. China was cracking down on intellectual property infringements of the big global brands, making things harder for the bootlegging trade. And the price of Chinese wholesale goods was rising as wages went up in a maturing economy and the exchange rate worsened for African currencies. China was becoming less attractive as a place of opportunity for Africans.

I was strolling along the road in the Xiaobei district, where the police presence had grown over the years, gently squeezing the African population through constant visa checks. I saw a dark-skinned African girl of about eight years in heated conversation – sorry, make that a heated monologue – with a policeman. He was standing in a sentry post on a traffic island in the middle of a quiet street; his face softened in silent amusement as the girl stood, legs akimbo like Superwoman, and gave him an earful in fluent Chinese. I began recording the scene on my phone. Realising she had found an audience, the kid got theatrical: hands now on hips and a twinkle in her eyes, she continued her rant at the cop, her eyes occasionally darting in my direction. When she finished, she marched off down the street. The policeman smiled a little and gestured to me to stop filming.

I had seen that same girl in the Tianxiu Building weeks earlier. She had sat with her legs straddled across a wheelie suitcase and was holding court with two Chinese vendors, this time in more genial tones, while her Muslim mother looked on. I wish I had caught up with that kid and been able to speak to her, find out more about her. Chances are she came from a Francophone country, meaning she probably spoke French, Mandarin and her indigenous tongue, perhaps Wolof or Mandinka. The kid's confidence with adults, her language skills and her overall moxie were a joy to behold. The life experiences she had accumulated were the stuff of Ivy League college application forms.

I posted the video of her rant on Facebook in the hope of getting a translation from one of my Mandarin- or Cantonese-speaking friends. Someone soon explained that the girl appeared to have been arguing with her mother, and the police officer was warning her not to disrespect her elders. The girl's response – the part of the conversation I witnessed – was to give him another piece of her mind.

A Nigerian-American friend of mine loved the Facebook video so much she commented beneath it: 'That girl is pure magic!' She was magic. But what did the future hold for this child, I wondered? Would her self-confidence and innate sense of justice be devoured by the Chinese cultural and political firewall? I wondered if she knew what powers she had. With skills like hers, the earth would feel like my oyster. But outcomes were different here in Guangzhou, the capital of the developing world and of low-level globalisation, where language skills, business know-how and life experience aren't monetised nearly enough. I gazed in admiration as the child marched down the street, her arms swinging in happy, girly defiance, and I smiled as she twisted her neck to glance back at me. We are resourceful people. She will use her language skills and confidence to navigate this tricky world. Something tells me she'll be alright.

XI

POSTSCRIPT

I finished writing this book during the COVID-19 pandemic. In the early days of the crisis, Africans in Guangzhou were scapegoated, accused of being prime vectors of this novel disease. The health commission began forcibly testing African nationals as part of a racially targeted campaign. A whiff of persecution pervaded, with ambulance sirens and quarantine replacing police sirens and prison cells. Africans were forced to self-isolate or be confined to designated hotels well before the rest of the population was ordered to stay indoors. In some cases the authorities entered Africans' homes to give tests. It was mandatory for all foreigners, they claimed, but Africans were the ones primarily targeted in the early days of the pandemic, even when they had tested negative, had not travelled recently or been in contact with COVID-19 sufferers. Alarms were installed outside some of their apartments. Some Africans were unceremoniously turfed out by their landlords and forced to sleep on the streets when hotels refused to check them in. Shops wouldn't serve them. Restaurants refused to take their orders: 'We've been informed that black people are not allowed to enter . . .' read the sign on the window of a McDonald's.

Given that most of Guangdong Province's imported cases of COVID-19 were Chinese citizens returning from abroad, these measures lacked any scientific rationale.

Infectious diseases, foreigners, immigration, disgust, fear of the disease-ridden outsider were all conflated in a primal panic that has been played out throughout history all over the world.

At the same time, thousands of kilometres away in the United States and the UK, the Chinese diaspora were receiving horrendous racist abuse as a result of the pandemic, which is believed to have originated in Wuhan. When the pandemic struck London, I was sharing an apartment with a British-Chinese friend. She and my other ethnic Chinese British friends had been insulted by strangers on the street ('You fucking Chinese cunt! You fucking brought it here, the lot of ya') and were extremely upset by it. Listening to her complaints about the vilification of her ethnic group while I busily chronicled the shit that Chinese people put Africans through was an awkward juxtaposition and a reminder that one man's victim is another man's tormentor.

Africans' treatment in Guangzhou during the Covid crisis brought a sobering clarity, as if any more were needed, over the imbalance between China and Africa, and how much Africa concedes to its Chinese immigrants compared to the paltry purchase that Africans have in the Middle Kingdom.

The pandemic in 2020 saw Africans depart China in their thousands, leaving the streets of Sanyuanli and Xiaobei almost deserted. But for people like the jeweller Ikem, who stayed put, there was a feeling that this was more than mere hibernation, that 'Little Africa' might never wake again. He described to me, via text messages, the quietness of his neighbourhood.

'Most actually returned home. We thought it was a few months' ordeal but it later turned out to be unending. You can visit Sanyuanli today and see only but a few (ten or a dozen) Africans, unlike before where they are in hundreds. It gets more serious that only few people with resident permits have been able to come in since this year.'

It's possible that Africans will never return to Guangzhou in the pre-Covid numbers, and that I had experienced the final years of a unique boom town that came and went, like a Californian gold-rush settlement consigned to the annals of history as an interesting, ephemeral experiment. But even if that turns out to be the case, the legacy will be lasting. China's exposure to Africans, whether it be listening to *Pop Idol*'s Lou Jing, receiving cardiac treatment from Koffi, or the DNA traces in the mixed children, will give Chinese people a broader sense of what is possible in this world. Exposure to foreigners, when it changes just one person's outlook, can make a difference and transform the lives of others in ways we can't always foresee.

FURTHER READING

BOOKS

Adams Bodomo, *Africans in China: Guangdong and Beyond*, Diasporic Africa Press, 2016

Howard French, China's Second Continent: How a Million Migrants Are Building a New Empire in Africa, Knopf, 2014

Emmanuel John Hevi, *An African Student in China*, Pall Mall Press, 1963

Charlotte Ikels, *The Return of the God of Wealth*, Stanford University Press, 1996

Shanshan Lan, *Mapping the New African Diaspora in China: Race and the Cultural Politics of Belonging*, Routledge, 2017

Gordon Mathews, *Globalization from Below: The World's Other Economy*, Routledge, 2012

Rob Schmitz, *Street of Eternal Happiness: Big City Dreams Along a Shanghai Road*, John Murray, 2016

Richard L. Williams, *At the Dawn of the New China*, Camphor Press, 2005

ARTICLES

Lily Kuo and Helen Davidson, '"They see my blue eyes then jump back" – China sees a new wave of xenophobia', *Guardian*, 29 March 2020: https://www.theguardian.com/world/2020/mar/29/china-coronavirus-anti-foreigner-feeling-imported-cases

Jenni Marsh, 'Afro-Chinese marriages boom in Guangzhou: But will it be "til death do us part"?', *South China Morning Post*, 2 July 2014: https://www.scmp.com/magazines/post-magazine/article/1521076/afro-chinese-marriages-boom-guangzhou-will-it-be-til-death

New Scientist, 'The truth about migration: how evolution made us xenophobes', 6 April 2016: https://www.newscientist.com/article/mg23030680-800-the-truth-about-migration-how-evolution-made-us-xenophobes/

Danny Vincent, 'Africans in China: We face coronavirus discrimination', BBC, 17 April 2020: https://www.bbc.co.uk/news/world-africa-52309414

ACKNOWLEDGEMENTS

First and foremost I'd like to thank the Miles Morland Scholarship and its judges Olufemi Terry, Muthoni Garland and Ellah Wakatama for awarding me the funds to travel to China. I owe an added debt of gratitude to Ellah who championed my manuscript and edited and shaped it into coherence. Big thanks also to Giles Foden for reading my initial draft, and to Ed Wall for copy-editing the final draft.

A thousand hand-kisses for my agent Elise Dillsworth and the folks at Canongate, particularly Rali Chorbadzhiyska, Leila Cruickshank and Anna Frame. Hat-tip to Helen Smith and Serena Wong for their help and support. And lastly, many thanks to my sister Zina and our dear, late mother Maria who was always the solid ground beneath my feet.